To Pat and
Best Wish-
Johnny Morris

THE FALL GUY

I was the double for Michael Caine and John Lennon

Johnny Morris

GLENEAGLE BOOKS

THE FALL GUY

I was the double for Michael Caine and John Lennon

by Johnny Morris

Edited by Nick Freeth

Cover designed by Phil Clucas

Thanks to Brian and Lynne Cahill

The Author asserts the Author's right to be identified in relation to the Work on
the title page in the following form: JOHNNY MORRIS

© Johnny Morris 2016

Published by Gleneagle Books Ltd, London, United Kingdom
www.gleneaglebooks.com

ISBN: 978-0-9932727-0-7

CONTENTS

LIST OF ILLUSTRATIONS

Between pages 48 and 49:

My father, 'Gentleman Jim' Morris, with my Uncle Arthur, who was a famous light heavyweight boxer.

An old photo of my father and one of my many half-brothers, James Jnr.

An illustrated card from my archive, giving details of my Uncle Arthur's impressive boxing career.

A damaged picture fragment showing my father and another man boxing blindfolded.

The passing-out parade after my National Service basic training.

Pictures from *The V.I.P.s* (1963), showing me and Dennis Price assisting Elizabeth Taylor as she leaves a helicopter.

Some of my own, previously unpublished photos, taken in May 1965 on the set of the second Beatles movie, *Help!*, at Cliveden House, near Maidenhead.

The Beatles' stand-ins in the studio.

Ringo Starr, George Harrison and Victor Spinetti taking a rest at Cliveden during the *Help!* shoot.

Setting up a scene for *Help!* in a field. I'm standing in the foreground, while director Dick Lester talks to John Lennon.

A scene from *The Ipcress File*, with me and Bill Sulley.

Me and Michael Caine in Hyde Park, during the making of *The Ipcress File*.

My photo of Michael, taken through a screen on the set of *The Ipcress File*.

The menu for the *Alfie* post-première party, held at the *Cockney Pride* restaurant in London's Jermyn Street on 24th March 1966.

On location for *Funeral in Berlin*.

With Mike on the frozen Finnish sea while we were making *Billion Dollar Brain*.

A studio shot from *Billion Dollar Brain*.

On location for *Deadfall* in Majorca, with Mike's co-star Giovanna Ralli.

Roy Pontin (wardrobe), Freddie Williamson (make-up), Michael Caine and me, photographed in Majorca during work on *Deadfall*.

The call sheet setting out the schedule for a day's work on *Deadfall*.

Dickie Graydon doing a stunt for *The Italian Job* with me.

Preparing for another *Italian Job* stunt: I'm at the wheel of a truck that's about to ram a door.

In Turin during work on *The Italian Job*.

Model Bianca Macias (Mike's then-girlfriend, later to become Bianca Jagger) visits the *Italian Job* set.

The robbers from *The Italian Job*, disguised as football supporters.

Between pages 88 and 89:

Some photographs of me from the 1960s, sent out to potential clients by the agent who handled my modelling assignments.

On location for *Play Dirty*, with director André de Toth and actress Vivian Pickles.

Me in costume alongside Michael Caine, who starred as Captain Douglas in *Play Dirty*.

Me and Michael outside his caravan (today's stars would be provided with much larger, more luxurious ones!) on location for *Play Dirty*.

Getting ready to shoot a scene for *Play Dirty*, alongside my old friend Kit West, a special effects artist and future Oscar winner.

Another *Play Dirty* photo: I'm relaxing at the wheel of a heavily laden Army truck.

On location for *Too Late The Hero* in the Philippines, with director Bob Aldrich.

Lance Percival, Ronnie Fraser and Michael Caine alongside me at Taipei Airport during a break from filming *Too Late The Hero*.

My certificate of membership for the 'Olongapoo Patrol,' signed by Mike and other stars from the cast of *Too Late The Hero*.

Two photos I took of Mike in costume as 'The Captain' from *The Last Valley*.

A picture of me in Newcastle, taken while I was working as the stunt arranger for *Get Carter*.

A light-hearted moment on the set of *Get Carter* in Newcastle, with me, Mike, and stunt man Derek Baker.

Jack Law and Billy Campbell of Greenmantle, the Scottish band I managed in the 1970s.

A signed photo of me with Sir Laurence Olivier, who starred alongside Michael Caine in *Battle of Britain* and *Sleuth*.

Photos taken during the shooting of *Sleuth*, including pictures of two stunts.

On the set of *Pulp* with Mickey Rooney.

Me and Don Siegel, the director of *The Black Windmill*.

Filming a stunt in a winery for *The Marseille Contract*.

A group of local kids in Kenya, photographed with me during shooting for *The Wilby Conspiracy*.

A signed photo of Sidney Poitier, who co-starred with Michael Caine in *The Wilby Conspiracy*.

Shakira Caine, Michael Caine, and Mike's agent Dennis Selinger with me and my wife Jean at a dinner party in Kenya after the end of shooting for *The Wilby Conspiracy*.

Two photos from the *Richmond & Twickenham Times*, showing the celebrations marking the opening of 'Phil Parkes Sports' in Twickenham on Thursday 22nd April 1976. (Reproduced by kind permission of the *Richmond & Twickenham Times*.)

Two photos of me, taken in 2014 by my friend Lynne Cahill.

PREFACE

The 1960s were recently voted the UK's favourite decade, and the adjectives often used to describe them—'swinging' and 'stylish,' but also 'turbulent' and 'iconoclastic'—sum up the enduring attraction of an era whose moods were memorably captured and preserved in music, literature and films. Bob Dylan was preaching to the converted when he sang *The Times They Are a-Changin'* in 1964; and Philip Larkin's poem *Annus Mirabilis* was able to pinpoint when "sexual intercourse began" by reference to the release date of the first Beatles LP the previous year.

The Fao Four represented one aspect of the 60s' 'vibe,' to adopt a term that was on everyone's lips back then. Another iconic product of the period was Michael Caine, who made his name with groundbreaking movies like *The Ipcress File* and *Funeral in Berlin*, and was to become a defining presence in British and international cinema. If you're an admirer of Caine and the Beatles, you'll already have encountered the work of Johnny Morris, though you may not recognise his name. Johnny was Caine's long-time stand-in, double, and stunt arranger; he also doubled for John Lennon in *A Hard Day's Night* and *Help!*, and was actively involved, behind the scenes and sometimes in front of the camera, with many other celebrated film productions of the 1960s and 70s. This is his autobiography: read on, and you'll learn a few things "not a lot of people know"...

To my wife Jean,

my daughter Victoria and her husband Harry,

my son Matthew and his wife Andrea,

my grandchildren Harry, Scarlett, Ruby, Max,

Joel and Freddie,

and my three great-grandchildren Louie,

Harrison and Violet.

1: MY EARLY LIFE AND MY PARENTS

I was born in 1934 in Shepherd's Bush, West London, close to the Lime Grove studios where I had my first real job. My father came from Fulham, and was one of about ten children; before I was born, he worked as a granite floor layer, like most of his family. He was the guv'nor on a big floor-laying job for the Peabody Trust at the Cleverly Estate in Shepherd's Bush, and went on to live in one of the properties there. He and my mother then moved to the flat in Devonport Road which was my childhood home; the Cleverly Estate was badly damaged by a V-2 rocket in February 1945.

They called my father 'Gentleman Jim' in Shepherd's Bush. He always wore a hat, and a stiff collar and tie. His collars were detachable ones, fastened with a stud, and he used to clean them by rubbing them with dry bread. Our whole family were smartly turned out, as you can see from the pictures of us taken when I was a kid: we must have had a few bob to dress like that. But my father didn't know how to stop gambling or drinking, and that was his downfall. He lost £3,000 at the dog track in the '30s—with that kind of money he could probably have bought six houses, and the landlord in Devonport Road offered to sell him the building containing our flat for £200, but he wasn't interested. He was a bookmaker as well as a gambler, and an associate of two powerful crime families: the Sabinis, and the Whites, who took over from them after the war. Dad worked for them on the racecourses: the head of the Sabini clan was known as 'Derby', and they controlled all the on-course gambling, with gangsters operating in pairs and targeting the punters. If somebody got lucky and had a win, one of these guys would jostle him and push his arm up as he was putting his money away, so that his 'other half' could get in and grab back the cash.

My father also ran his own illegal off-course operation on the Goldhawk Road. He was down on the corner taking bets every day, and he paid two plain clothes police officers up to £25 a week to mind him and tip him off if there was going to be a raid. He used to send me up to Goldhawk Road station every night to pick up the *Evening News*, the *Star* and the *Evening Standard*, which contained the racing results. He and the punters went to the races by coach: a firm called Bingley Brothers ran services from Hammersmith Broadway to the various meetings.

My father played cards too, and would travel to Newcastle with one of my half-brothers for games of Brag and poker. They made a lot of money, but they were 'at it,' and got barred from going back after being found out. Dad taught one of my cousins, Ted Morris, to play Brag: Ted's my half-brother's son, and I'm his uncle, though I'm younger than him! He says that when he went into the Army, he always did well out of the game.

My own uncle, Arthur Morris (my father's brother) was a successful light heavyweight boxer, based in Fulham. I was too young to know him well, but I've heard that he fought against many other big names (including Dido Plumb, Ted Bryant and Gunner Moir), often gave exhibition matches at major venues such as Earls Court and Olympia, and even took on the American World Champion, Jim Jeffries, in a bout at London's Royal Aquarium, where the Methodist Central Hall now stands, in 1899.

We were the only family in the street that had a car. In fact, we had two of them—an ex-police Wolseley, and a Riley shooting-brake—but they just sat outside the house, as my father couldn't drive. He'd bought them through another of my half-brothers, this one on my mother's side. His name was Pat Connolly, and he was a petty officer in the Navy. Pat drove them sometimes, but he also had a motor-bike and sidecar, and I got more rides in his sidecar than I ever did in the cars.

My father was a bit of a lad. Although I'm an only child, I've got as many as eight half-brothers and sisters on his side of the family, and I know that he may have had two previous wives before marrying my mother. One day, when a sister-in-law of his was passing a register office near the King's Road in Chelsea, she caught sight of him posing for photographs on the steps after yet another marriage—who to, I don't know! She reported him, and he was convicted of bigamy and did time for it.

My mother knew about all this, like everybody else, and there were quite a few rows between my parents, especially when my father came home late after she'd got his dinner ready. He would shout at her, and then throw the dinner so that you'd see the plate hit the wall and slip down. He never hit me: in fact, later on, as I got older, I actually turned on him, and we came to blows when I stood up for my mother. She was a very shrewd lady, who worked as a barmaid at exhibitions and concerts in places like Olympia and the Albert Hall. She'd sometimes bring back cakes and other leftover treats from the events there, which was lovely. Her family, the Connollys, were Irish, and she had an odd little dent in her forehead as the result of a childhood injury she'd received in Ireland. She'd jumped onto the back of a horse and cart, and the driver had turned round and caught her with his whip. There was a dart on its end, which left a scar and a little hole. Her sister, Florrie, lived in Colchester, and she had two brothers: one in New Zealand, the other a Catholic priest in Canada.

Our basement flat in Devonport Road had a front room, a back room, a kitchen, and a toilet—that was all. My mother and father slept in the back room, and my single bed was in the other one, where there was a wood fire to keep me warm. The kitchen had a small stove, and a concrete basin in the corner for washing clothes, with a fire underneath to heat the water. My mother would get the garments clean by plunging them up and down with a stick as they soaked, and put them through a mangle afterwards. Bigger weekly washes were done in the massive machines at the Public Baths, just behind where we lived. All the different families' clothes would go in together, and we had name-tags sewn onto them so we could tell which were ours.

There were first- and second-floor flats in the Devonport Road house, and I remember the people on the top floor, Mr. and Mrs. Clark, used to eat horse-meat, which had an odd, sweet smell when it was cooking. Lots of people ate horse-meat in those days, and it was sold in Shepherd's Bush Market. There'd be daily deliveries of milk to the flats, and among the other tradesmen who'd call regularly or ply their trade in the street outside were the coal merchant, the rag-and-bone man, and a guy who went around ringing a bell and selling muffins.

Our flat was a diabolical place to live, and there wasn't much to do there, though we did have a British Relay Wireless—a cabled-up box with a three-way switch and a loudspeaker, through which we could listen to radio programmes. Later on, my father got a television, too:

it had a stand about twice the size of its tiny screen, and we put a magnifying glass in front of it to make its picture look bigger. The thing I hated most about the flat was the toilet under its stairs: I still get nightmares about that horrible little room! The only good thing about it was that I could develop and print my own photos there. I'd learned the basics of photography from one of our neighbours, and I had a half-plate camera that could be used as an enlarger. I kept dishes of developing and fixing chemicals in the toilet, and later on, I developed rolls of film there too. I enjoyed that, but hated having to spend so much time by myself in the flat while my mother was working late, and my father was out drinking or whatever. I'd often go outside in the dark, at maybe 10 o'clock, or even 12 o'clock at night, and stand on the corner waiting for my parents to come home.

Every day, I used to go round to the Public Baths for a hot bath. From the waiting room, you'd be called into one of the cubicles, each of which had numbers, and was fitted with fold-down seats attached to the wall. The taps, outside in the corridor, were controlled by an attendant who'd fill up the bath, and walk up and down adding hot and cold water when you asked for it. For a laugh, I used to give the wrong cubicle number when calling out for more hot water. If I was in Number 3, I'd say, "Can I have a drop more hot in Number 7?"—and all of a sudden, you'd hear the guy in Number 7 shouting, "Hold up! Hold up!" because it was burning him! When you got out of the bath, there was a slotted wooden tray to stand on, and you'd dry yourself with a rotten, rough old towel that they'd give you, along with a very small bar of soap, while you were waiting to go in. As I mentioned earlier, families would do their weekly laundry in the big washing machines installed in another part of the building.

During the war, everyone in our house shared a brick-built air-raid shelter. Its roof was solid concrete, which must have been about two feet thick, and there were bunks inside; but my father would never get into it, and if the alarm sounded, he'd just hide under the bed. I remember the doodlebugs coming across. When their engines cut out, you knew they were going to dip and hit somewhere. We were pretty lucky, because no bombs dropped on our street, though quite a few fell round about. All our windows had to be taped up to stop the glass blasting in if a bomb came down, and the air-raid wardens would often call round to check you were observing the blackout. They were very strict, and would be sure to tell you off if any lights were showing.

When the air-raids started to get really bad, I was evacuated. They sent me to a couple of places: I don't remember where the first one was, but it was filthy, and I caught scabies. My mother came down and had a go at the people there, because I was smothered in sores, and she took me away. I finished up near Calne in Wiltshire, along with other girls and boys from London. I liked the country life, and worked a lot on the farm—especially with pigs, of all things—and I used to drive a horse and cart, which was fun. My parents sent me money, and gave extra cash to Mrs. Ruttey, the lady who was looking after me. They also bought me a speed bike, which was great for racing round the streets there, and I was always well-kept, clothes-wise. I stayed in touch with my parents by letter. My mother came down to see me once in a while, but my father never did.

I began to enjoy myself so much there that at one stage I didn't really want to come back to London, which was strange. In fact, I was the final evacuee to leave the village at the end of the war—and because I was a Londoner, and the last one there, I got picked on by the local children. One time, when they were chasing me in the street, I turned round and hit one of them, and made his nose bleed. I knew I was in trouble then, so I ran back to Mrs. Ruttey's house, where I was living, and hid under the sink in the kitchen. The mum and dad of the boy I'd hit were after me. They came knocking at the door, saying, "Where is he? Where's that Londoner?" Mrs. Ruttey didn't know I was under the sink! It all died down...and soon afterwards, I came back to London, where there were bombed buildings all over the place. It was quite a change from what I'd left behind.

I went to a couple of schools in Shepherd's Bush, both called St. Stephen's: a Church of England school on the Uxbridge Road, and a Roman Catholic school in Rylett Road that had a playground on top of its roof. It was there that I got caned on the backside—in front of the whole school, which was a punishment in itself—when I was about 13. I'd been playing truant a lot, and an inspector caught me on a bomb site around the Askew Road. I was mucking about there with a couple of friends. They got away, and I could see the inspector coming, and tried to dodge him, but he caught me, reported me, and I was given a beating.

About the same time, I had some trouble with one of my neighbours, an older kid who shared my surname (though we weren't related), and lived with his mum about four or five doors away from us in Devonport Road. He was a lot bigger than me, over six feet in height, and he used to pick on me and bully me. All my friends, boys and girls, were around in the street when he did it. I got so annoyed that one day I just snapped. I rushed down into our flat, where I had an air-gun, and came back out and fired at him! Everyone ran for their lives when they saw me with the gun, and the guy didn't bother me any more after that.

I was always sporty as a kid, and played every night in the street, using a tennis ball for a football. Round the corner from where we lived were blank walls with cricket stumps and goalposts painted onto them, and my friends and I built our own scooters and wheeled trolleys out of the junk that was lying around everywhere after the war. We used ball-bearings for wheels: to make a scooter, we'd take a plank of wood, cut a V in it to insert a ball-bearing, and add a T-piece whose handles you could steer with, another piece of wood at the back, and wheels either side. Our trolleys were like wheeled carts you could sit on and steer, with someone else pushing you. Like the scooters, they were easy to construct, and great fun. I also went over to Perivale (about five miles to the west) on my bike to go horse-riding three or four times a week; I'd have to clean out the stables and groom the horses afterwards, and was shown how to. When I'd gained a bit more experience as a rider, I'd visit Richmond Park, where you could hire a polo pony. They were wonderfully manoeuvrable, and could turn on a sixpence...but you had to be careful not to pull them left or right too quickly, or you'd run the risk of being thrown off!

People in the street then were very friendly, though there was a bit of rivalry between 'Bush boys' and lads from Hammersmith and Fulham, which were close by. These were all tough neighbourhoods, but you could leave your front door open, and not be scared of walking down the street and getting mugged; and people weren't being stabbed every day of the week. If there was a fight in the street, it was a proper fight, a fist fight, and the guys would stand round watching, like it was a boxing ring. I'll never forget that my father once said to me: "Son, if you're in a fight with people watching you, and you think the guy's getting the better of you, give someone in the crowd a dig to get them involved...because while they're all going for each other, you can get away!" Things weren't like they are now, when if someone goes down they'll be kicking him in the head. Back then, once he was on the ground, that was it—the other guy had won. Not like today!

There was plenty of crime around. My father was able to pull something off when he discovered that a government warehouse in White City had stocks of Longines and Omega watches, specially imported for use by pilots and the military. There must have been a hell of a lot of them, because he arranged for quite a few to 'go missing,' and made a good deal of money out of it! Of course, the balloon went up, and the Old Bill came round to our flat in Devonport Road to search for the watches. I think there were two or three carloads of police, and I remember them digging out our coal cellar—which was full of coal—and going right through the house. But of course, they couldn't find anything, as my father had already been tipped off. They took him down to Askew Road Police Station to be interviewed, and also started questioning me, though I knew nothing about what he'd been up to. I must have been 13 or 14 at the time, and my mother went mad at them and shouted, "Don't you *dare* question my boy." They never found the watches, and didn't charge my father. One of the senior policemen down at Askew Road, who obviously knew him well, once said to him, "Jim, as you get older, you get wiser..." What he meant was that it was hard to prove anything against crafty, experienced law-breakers like my dad.

After I came back from the country, I had a pocket-money job on a toy stall at Shepherd's Bush Market. I'd been learning woodwork at school—I left at 14—and had thought about becoming a carpenter; but instead, I was taken on as a 'call-boy' at the studios at Lime Grove, which were being used by BBC Television. The money wasn't very good (about £1 10s. [£1.50] a week), but the work there helped to nurture my interest in show business. My job was to fetch the artists from their dressing rooms when they were needed on the set, and I got fascinated by the atmosphere. I loved the sets, and enjoyed watching people doing their jobs—especially the cameramen with their huge cameras. The show I was working on starred Petula Clark and Norman Wisdom; I was very keen on drumming at the time, and the drummer in the orchestra for the show was teaching me to play, but I didn't follow it through.

The other big influence on me at that time was Sulgrave Boys Club in Goldhawk Road, where I used to play table tennis and snooker every night. The club also had football and cricket teams, as well as a bar that sold soft drinks, tea, and hot chocolate instead of alcohol. You could buy nice cheese rolls and hot pies there too. The guy who ran it lived on the premises, kept the whole place clean and well-ordered—there was never any trouble—and looked after the bar with the food and drink. He was the main man, and he and his wife were like a family to us, and knew all the boys. There was rivalry between the Sulgrave Club and the Rugby Club in Notting Hill, and we'd have boxing, football, cricket, table tennis and snooker matches with them. Without the club, I might have got into more trouble, like my father and his family. Sometimes, when I wasn't working, I'd hang around the snooker hall in King Street, Hammersmith, where there was gambling and other things going on. But being into sport and belonging to the club helped to save me from all that.

I didn't stay at the BBC very long. At that time, I never said to myself, "This could be the place to be." You didn't think about careers in those days: you just wanted to have a nice suit, and go out and enjoy yourself. And I was able to do that, because my mother was working at major venues where I could get to see lots of big sports and music events. I remember going to Earls Court in 1948 for the Aquashow, starring Johnny Weissmuller, who was Tarzan. I saw heavyweight boxer Joe Louis there the same year, when he was doing exhibition matches. My mother actually took me up to meet him: I recall his trainer saying to him, "Shake hands with the boy, Joe," and he just did what he was told—like a dummy! I didn't get a photo of that, but I have got a signed one of Joe Louis himself. Mum was also involved with concerts at the Albert Hall, where there were performances by some of the top American bands.

Because my family had a bit of money, they spoilt me in one way, as I wasn't made to stick at a job. They never said to me, "You've got to do this and you've got to do that," but just let me do what I wanted. I went on to work in menswear shops, and in all sorts of other jobs. For a while, I was employed by Barkers, the big department store in Kensington High Street, to take photographs of the children visiting Father Christmas there. I was also taken on at a building company, as a plumber's mate. I didn't meet the plumber I'd been teamed up with until I went out on my first job with him. It was at a school in Wandsworth, where we were renewing the toilet pan in the headmistress's office. I asked the plumber what we had to do, and he told me to sponge out all the water in the pan, which was old, and had horrible brown stains in it. I said, "No, not me!" and I walked off and went home. Not surprisingly, I didn't last long there, and I never got paid, either. I had much more fun, a few years later, with the fruit barrow a mate and I used to run outside the Shepherd's Bush Empire theatre. We did a roaring trade with the audiences there in the evenings, but we didn't have a licence, and had to keep moving on to avoid trouble with the police.

When I was 18 in 1952, I got called up for two years' National Service. A lot of my friends had gone into the forces before me, and some of them were in the Royal Artillery. When they came home on leave, I'd ask them, "What's it like?" and they'd say, "Oh, terrific! We're driving about in trucks and having lots of fun." I liked the sound of all that, and put my name down for the Royal Artillery. But because of my background, being basically a labourer, they put me in the infantry, and I joined the 1st Battalion Royal Irish Fusiliers. They shipped me off to Ireland to do my eight weeks' training in Armagh, where the sergeants threatened us that if we didn't sign up for three years, we couldn't go home on leave. But at that age, I didn't care a monkey's about anybody, and I wouldn't have it. I told them, "There's no way I'm signing on for three years," and in fact, they didn't force us, so I was able to take my leave in London.

After returning to Ireland, I was posted to Hanover in Germany, and while I was there, I damaged my cartilage through playing football, and had to have it taken out. At the time, my father wasn't too well—he was suffering with his chest and what-have-you—and I thought, "I need to get back home." The only way I was able to manage that was by taking advantage of my injury, and I started to get up to silly things once I'd had the operation. I didn't do the exercises the physios told me to do, and as a result, one of my legs is still thinner than the other. And I used to jump from the stairs in the barracks, and land on my bad leg. It swelled right up, and they sent me back to England—to Netley Hospital in Southampton, an Army hospital that put me through a régime just like a physical training instruction course to get my leg better. I'd hoped to be discharged from the Army with the injury, but when I realised that it wasn't going to happen, my next move was to go and see the Roman Catholic padre. I told him, "I'm worried about my family, my father's not too well." He got me a compassionate posting back from Germany to Hounslow barracks in West London. From there, I was able to go home to Shepherd's Bush in my uniform, get changed into civvies, go out of an evening, stay the night at home, then put my uniform back on and return to the barracks in time for parade at 8 a.m. the next day.

It was strange sleeping at home while still being in the Army, and things could have worked out a whole lot worse for me. This was the time of the Korean War, and one of our sister regiments, the Ulster Rifles, was suffering heavy casualties in the fighting. They'd sent to our regiment for replacements while I was in Germany, and there had been so many volunteers—including me—that they'd had to put our names into a hat to select who'd be posted to the Far East. But I was never chosen (thank goodness!), and at Hounslow, I worked in the officers' mess, laying the tables and waiting on them. It was a great job, because we'd get good food, the same as the officers had; but I fell out with one of the other guys there, and we had a fight in the mess. One of the officers came in and caught us, and that was it—I was locked up in a cell at the barracks, and charged.

After that, they put me to work on the coal wagon, delivering coal to all the married service families nearby. We also took coal supplies to the Royal Military School of Music at Kneller Hall in Whitton. The wagon was driven by a civilian called Taffy, and when we were heading up to get the coal from the Army depot on Hounslow Heath (we had to shovel it onto the back of the open truck), I noticed a pen on the side of the road, surrounded by barbed wire, containing corrugated steel panels for Anderson shelters and other valuable stuff. Taffy told me that some of the prisoners from London jails came to do their daily work there. Seeing these convicts through the fence gave me an idea, so I asked Taffy to stop the truck so I could have a chat with them. They gave me a bit more information about what was inside the pen, and I realised I could make some money selling it, so I said, "Any chance of doing a deal? If I get you some cigarettes, can you throw over what we want?" And they did! For a while, it was a nice little racket, with them lobbing the gear over the fence, and me selling it, but eventually someone must have shopped us. One day, when Taffy and I were driving up to get the coal, some guys suddenly jumped out from the ditches beside the road—there were no houses nearby, just the pen with the barbed wire on one side of the road, and open ground on the other—and stopped us. We'd been caught by the SIBs, the Special Investigation Branch, who'd been lying in wait for us there. I was put on a charge, but I got off it somehow, though how, I don't know.

There was another incident on the coal trucks. Quite a few soldiers were doing the same job as I was, and I had some trouble with a Scotsman from the Black Watch. He said something to me while we were loading up our lorry, and we ended up having a terrible row. I don't remember what it was over, but once again, I lost it and gave him a dig. I was put back inside again—military detention for fighting on duty—though I was only banged up for about two weeks at Hounslow, and I left the Army soon after. They were very lenient with me, really. I think it was because I was on a compassionate posting, due to my father's bad health.

He suffered a lot with his chest, and the smog we used to have in London made it a whole lot worse. It was sometimes so thick that if you were on a bus, you'd have to get out and walk along the edge of the pavement, so the driver could spot where the kerb was: you couldn't see six feet in front of you. I don't think the drink helped my father either, and he used to smoke and take snuff, which I thought was a horrible habit. He'd carry a little tin of it, and shake it out on the back of his hand to sniff it.

He died when I was about 30, and my mother survived him by a good few years. Later on, I managed to get her out of Devonport Road, and into a top-floor flat in Boscombe Road; I thought it was safer for her there. After that, I got her moved to Twickenham, near where I was living at the time. We found her a nice top flat in a terraced house, with a friendly couple downstairs, and she stayed there till the end of her days. She loved watching snooker on the television, and she kept a bottle down the side of her chair. I'd ask her, "What's in that bottle, Mum?" "Oh, it's Coca-Cola," she'd say, but it wasn't—it was port! She'd have it by her side, and drink it while she was watching TV. Mum passed away in 1985, and the people downstairs rang me at Shepperton Studios, where I was working, when she died. Of course, I left the set and rushed straight round...and she'd gone.

2: GETTING STARTED IN THE MOVIES, AND MY FIRST FILMS WITH MICHAEL CAINE

I'd just come out of the Army when I met Jean, my wife-to-be. Back then, I used to knock around the snooker hall at Hammersmith, and I got to know her through some friends. She was a typist, secretary and comptometer operator (comptometers were mechanical calculators that were eventually replaced by electronic ones), and she worked for one of the bosses at Joseph Lyons, the famous catering company with offices near Olympia. Her mother and father had both died—her father first; her mother died of cancer when Jean was quite small—so she was living with an auntie in Bedford Park, near Turnham Green. When we were courting, I didn't have a car, and often had to catch the last bus back to Shepherd's Bush from Bedford Park. Sometimes I missed it, and had to walk or run several miles to get home. I used to do a lot of running in those days, and was very fit!

By the time Jean and I got married in 1957, I was working at Olympia, where I'd started out in a funny old job, but one that a lot of people wanted. It involved cleaning out the gangways, sweeping up, and providing security on the doors when the exhibitions were on. They'd give you a brown coat, and you'd sit at the exits to stop unauthorised people getting in. Then I became an electrician's mate— a very good job, working with a qualified electrician to provide lighting for the exhibitions at Olympia and Earls Court. Everyone doing this electrical work knew each other, and I remember some friends of ours, two brothers called Johnny and Benny Lee, taking on a private job for a guy who'd bought an old chapel off the Goldhawk Road, a couple of streets from where I lived. He was turning the place into a studio to make commercials, and after he'd hired Johnny and Benny to fix up the lights in the offices, he said to them, "How would you like to light the sets as well?" They told him they didn't know how to do that, and he replied, "Well, you'll soon learn, won't you?" Which they did! They went on to form one of the biggest lighting companies in the film industry, Lee Lighting. I worked on the site near Goldhawk Road, along with several of my friends. Johnny and Benny employed us on a number of other jobs, and we helped them build up their stock of lamps and other equipment for movie sets.

My next job was with Mole-Richardsons, an American firm that was the leading name in the film lighting business before the Lees came along. As before, I was an electrician's mate: electricians themselves would handle the technical side of the jobs, like connections, outputs and maintenance, while we would lay the cables, get the lights (to do this, we had to know about all the different types, and how they were used), set them up, and operate them on gantries or down on the ground. 'Brutes' were the biggest of all the lights. They had two carbon arcs burning inside which would sometimes need replacing, and you'd have to keep looking through a little window to make sure there was the right distance between the carbons, so they didn't fade away or burn out. Sometimes the Brutes would be shining down on the set from a gantry, but when they were used at ground level, they'd be mounted on massive wheeled tripods. There was a handle to push them up or lower them down, and you'd need to climb up on steps to reach the window through which you could check the carbons. At the other end of the scale from Brutes were 'Pups'—small, ground-level lights that were used as fill-ins, depending on what the lighting cameraman wanted. There were lots of other kinds of lamps, like Fresnels (the smallest of these were nicknamed 'inkies'), which have special lenses to provide wider, softer-edged beams of light, and battery-powered 'sun guns'...but whatever the lighting cameraman asked for, you had to get it for him, because he was the main man. When you worked on lighting, you'd be employed on a film, from beginning to end, at one of the big studios hired by the movie companies—places like Pinewood, Borehamwood, Merton Park, Shepperton, and Bray. As they all had so many stages, they could accommodate several different films at the same time: a single one wouldn't occupy a whole studio unless it was something like a James Bond production.

Because it got very hot up on the gantries with the Brutes, we always used to look forward to working on Walt Disney pictures. Unlike other production companies, they would lay on a supply of orange juice in the studio, and it was nice to come down and have a cold drink during the breaks. In fact, it was when I was lighting the sets for a Disney film, *Greyfriars Bobby*, made at Shepperton and released in 1961, that one of my friends, Ronnie McWorth, who'd started out working at exhibitions like me, suggested I should get in front of the camera, initially for crowd and background scenes. To do this, you had to be a member of the Film Artistes' Association (the FAA), which was very hard to get into, but Ronnie was pally with the guys that ran it at that time. He asked me if I fancied it, and I said, "Yes, great!" For these onscreen jobs, you needed a good wardrobe, including things like dinner jackets and smart suits, though obviously there were occasions when they'd hire stuff for you to wear. I was always keen on looking good, and used to go to tailors like Levy's in Hammersmith to have my suits made up. They'd bring out swatches of material—birdseye and hopsack were especially popular in the early 1960s—and you could choose single- or double-breasted jackets, specify the number of buttons, and display a handkerchief in your top pocket to look really smart. Your clothes were complemented by your hairstyle, and barbers would display photographs of classic cuts such as the 'Tony Curtis,' 'D.A.' ('duck's arse'!) and 'Boston'; my friends and I would visit different barber's shops in Hammersmith to change from one style to another. And after a cut, we always had a friction—a massage that improves the circulation in your scalp, and feels wonderful. The lotions they used for them ('Blue Orchid,' 'Pashana') had lovely, distinctive smells.

When you first appear as an extra, you don't get regular work until people start asking for you, so it was fortunate that I was still able to do set lighting whenever I wanted. But luckily, one or two first assistant directors took a shine to me, and would use me in the crowd whenever they were doing a film. As a result, I became part of a circle of people who could be relied upon to do a job. The dressing rooms we all used were often looked after by ex-boxers, guys like Ted 'Kid' Lewis (the former world welterweight champion), Jack 'Kid' Berg (the 'Whitechapel Windmill'), and Len Harvey (who'd been British champion in three separate categories: middleweight, light heavyweight and heavyweight). With them keeping guard, you could be sure that nobody would try and steal anything.

Sometimes there were auditions for the film parts: once again, a first or second assistant director would put your name down for them, and that's how I and many others moved up to being stunt men and women. It was like another jump in your career, another side of the business, and my first experience of it was in the *Carry On* movies, where they'd want people to tumble about, fall off the backs of horses and carts, and things like that. I went on to do stunts for Steve McQueen in *The War Lover* (1962), which was shot in black and white at various locations around south-east England, and I also started working as a stand-in and a double. I got these jobs because I was the same size, height, and colour as quite a few actors, and if no one had already been hired to stand in or double for them when a film was being set up, a suitable person would be needed.

When you 'stand in,' you have to watch the rehearsals for a scene, and observe the actor's movements very closely. Then he'll go off, and the lighting cameraman will light the set with you taking his place. It'd be very tiring for the actor to hang about for all that, so he only comes back when they're ready to shoot the scene. If you don't watch carefully, hit the right spots, and copy the artist's movements exactly, the lighting and the camera angles won't be right, and they'll really have a go at you! The lights themselves used to be a problem, too: the electricians were meant to shout out when they were going to turn a powerful lamp onto you, because you could be dazzled or even have your eyes damaged.

'Doubling' is appearing on-camera in place of an actor, mostly for the action parts, where you'll be doing things that are too risky for the artists to perform themselves. You might take part in other scenes as well as stunts: I recall doubling for Michael Caine in a kissing scene during *Alfie*, which came out in 1966—they used my Vauxhall Velox in that movie too—and thinking, "This is nice!" When you're doubling, you've got to know how an actor uses his hands, and be able to copy his walk and the way he carries himself, so no one can tell that it isn't him in the shot. It's interesting work, but you have to be on your toes. Among the big names I doubled for was the Irish actor Stephen Boyd: that was thanks to Kip Gowans, an assistant director who was married to American actress Lee Remick, and who gave me a good deal of work. Later on, I stood in, doubled, and did stunts for leading players in quite a few television series as well. I worked on *Gideon's Way* (where I stood in for Derren Nesbitt), and in the early 1970s I sometimes doubled for Roger Moore in *The Persuaders!* (which also starred Tony Curtis) and *The Saint*. Roger usually had a guy called Les Crawford to do his doubling and stunting, but when Les wasn't available, they'd call on me. And doubling can lead to you being called upon to do 'front work,' where you're appearing alongside the artists. I was hired by a first assistant director to help Elizabeth Taylor out of a helicopter in *The V.I.P.s* (1963), and I drove the vintage Rolls-Royce in *Those Magnificent Men In Their Flying Machines* (1965). I got that job because I had a driving certificate from Rolls, who'd provided one of their showcase cars to the production, and insisted that only someone they'd certified should be allowed behind its wheel.

When I was starting out, you never received onscreen credits for standing in or doubling; in fact, it wasn't until I appeared in *The Italian Job* (1969) with Michael Caine that I was credited as a stand-in (though I did get a mention, three years earlier, for playing a 'Sotheby's assistant' in *The Wrong Box*: see later). Nowadays, everybody—even drivers and caterers—gets acknowledged on a movie's closing titles...which can sometimes take five minutes or more to show as a result!

Despite the lack of credits, though, I had quite a few interesting early jobs. One of the most exciting of them was being John Lennon's double on the first two Beatles films, *A Hard Day's Night* (1964) and *Help!* (1965), both of which were directed by Dick Lester. I auditioned, along with three of my friends, and the four of us stood in and doubled for John, Paul McCartney, George Harrison and Ringo Starr in both pictures. The Beatles were great to work with, though George was more laid back and shy than the others, and didn't come forward quite as much. The fans who followed them everywhere were crazy, and we often had to act as decoys for the real Beatles on location shoots at concert halls and railway stations. We'd be dressed as them, and would leave by the front door, while the boys themselves would get out round the back—there was no other way they could escape! I remember that for one of the movies, we were filming in the street in Ealing where my sister-in-law lived. She had two daughters, and said, "Next time Paul has his hair cut, could you get some of it for us?" Which I did...I gave them a few locks of his hair for them to keep. Back then, I don't think any of us realised just how famous the band would become. In 1965, I approached Sidney Stanford, a big-name tailor in Shepherd's Bush Green, told him I was working with the

Beatles, and asked him if we could do a deal, get the four of them to visit his shop and have their suits made there...but he turned me down flat: simply didn't want to know! A few years later, I'm sure he'd have changed his tune.

The group never really altered during the time I worked with them, and John and Paul, whom I got to know best, were very friendly. When we were filming *Help!*, there was a scene where Paul was made to look like a midget alongside an enormous fibreglass boot that was specially built for the set. John said to me, "Cor! I don't half like that boot!" so I told him I'd try and get it for him. When I found out we wouldn't be needing it again for the film, I arranged for it to be delivered to the house in Weybridge where he was living with his first wife, Cynthia. I had to ride on the back of the open-top lorry when we transported the boot from the studio, holding onto it so it wouldn't topple off. John put it in his driveway, and when you came in through the gates, the first thing you'd see would be this huge boot. He was very pleased with it. He also asked for my help when the Beatles were staying at a hotel near Bath during some location shooting for *Help!* I was with them at a party in a room up on the fourth floor when someone's head suddenly appeared at the window: a fan had shinned up a drainpipe, and was looking in at us. John said to me, "Get rid of him!" and I did—though I don't recall exactly how I managed it!

I had another small but memorable film role during this period— the part of the young woodchopper in *The Evil of Frankenstein* (1964), a Hammer horror movie made at Bray Studios in Berkshire. It starred Peter Cushing, who was a lovely man. In the story, I get taken away by a monster (played by a wrestler from New Zealand called Kiwi Kingston) to the place where Baron Frankenstein is going to cut my heart out. Peter Cushing was so gentle when he was marking up my chest before pretending to make his incisions; he said to me, "I'm not really going to do it, you know." That bit of the film was painless, but other parts turned out to be pretty unpleasant. There was a scene where I was being carried off to Frankenstein's lair, and had to hang limp over the monster's shoulder, which dug into my stomach and hurt like hell—especially after the four takes we needed to get it right! And the movie also featured my first solo stunt. After my character's heart had been removed, I was dumped, head first, through a trapdoor and into the swimming pool which was underneath the set, with a gap of about a foot between the surface of the water and the studio floor. I was meant to stay in the pool until they said, "Cut," but it was bitterly cold, and filthy dirty: there were dog-ends and all kinds of other muck in it, and when I was chucked in, I came straight back up again, like a porpoise. The director, Freddie Francis, was furious. "Cut! Cut! Cut!" he shouted. "What's the matter?" I told him how cold it was, and we did another take and got the shot. But when I came out of the pool, I just couldn't stop shivering—and they had to try and get me warm again, because I needed to stay and finish the scene. There was a nurse on the set, who wrapped me in blankets, and did her best to make me feel better, but the director couldn't have cared less.

Around the same time as this, I was doing some sword-fighting and stunting on a period-piece film called *She* (released in 1965) when I heard they were auditioning for a stand-in and double for Michael Caine in *The Ipcress File*. I didn't know Michael then, but Jean and I had seen him in *Zulu* (1964), and I'd been very impressed. I thought he stood out, had a good part, and looked great, and remember saying to Jean, "I think I could double for him." So, as soon as I heard there was going to be an audition, I left the studios, got in the car, and drove over to the building in Soho, in central London, where it was being held at an office on the top floor. I parked, and rushed up the stairs to a room where about twenty guys were already sitting, waiting to be called in. Over in the corner was a door to an inner office, which opened just as I arrived. The production manager for the movie came out and called "Next!", so I went from one door to the other, and headed straight inside before anyone else knew what was happening. So now I was face-to-face with the director (Sidney J. Furie) and a few other people sitting at a table. They had a look at my height and colour, and asked me some questions about other work that I'd done, and whether I knew how to fight and throw myself about. I gave them my answers—and got the job.

Pretty soon, we were shooting the movie (which also featured Nigel Green and Gordon Jackson), and I found Michael Caine very good to work with, though of course we were only starting to get familiar with each other, and he didn't know what I was capable of. After all, I'd only been chosen to be his double and stand-in for this one production, and if he and I hadn't hit it off, I wouldn't have been on his next film; it was as simple as that. But as it happened, I liked him, he liked me, and about six weeks in, he took me aside and said, "We're getting on so well that I'd like you to stay with me, and work with me all the time—and as I get bigger, you'll get bigger." Those were his exact words. I told him that I'd need to think about it, because I was working with John Lennon; Michael may have been a bit surprised, but he said, "Yes, alright." But when I got back home that evening, I talked it over with Jean, thought about it some more, and said to her: "The Beatles aren't actors. They're a fantastic group, but I don't think they're going to do many films." So I decided to accept Michael's offer, and when we went in on the set the next day, I said, "Yes, I'd love to work with you." That's how it all started...and that's the way it went for twenty-odd films, including some of the very finest British pictures of the 1960s and early 70s.

The Ipcress File came out in 1965: I had a small part of my own in it, as one of the heavies who drove a Mercedes. A couple of other heavies were needed as well, and I was able to get two of my friends in to play them. My second movie with Michael was *Alfie*, made in 1965, and released the following year. He had the title role, and though I still didn't know him 100%, I was starting to establish myself as his regular man, and did all his stunt work. It was quite a fun film, with a great cast, including Shelley Winters, Millicent Martin, Julia Foster, Jane Asher, Shirley Anne Field, Vivien Merchant, Eleanor Bron, Denholm Elliott and Alfie Bass. The director was Lewis Gilbert. Much of it was shot around Twickenham, and for the nursing home scene with Alfie Bass, we used York House, where Richmond Borough Council had its offices: it's a fantastic, very old building, with grounds out the back going down to the River Thames.

Shelley Winters was especially lovely to work with, and very funny. I remember the Boat Race was on while we were shooting, and everybody on the set wanted to know the result. When it came through—a win for Oxford by four lengths—Shelley said, "Only four lengths...among eight men," and the whole stage just roared! Michael couldn't stop laughing, and the technicians were in stitches. I shouldn't think she knew anything about boat races, but she just came out with it.

It's important to realise just how much Michael changed the whole of the film industry in those early years. The business was very toffee-nosed back then, and as a newcomer from south-east London, he was like somebody from another world. You could say that he, as well as the characters like Harry Palmer that he played, were classic products of the 1960s—a period when anything seemed possible, and anybody with talent and charisma could succeed, regardless of their social background. His cockney accent was nothing like the posh voices of the longer-established actors; he brought that in, and Bob Hoskins and other people followed in his footsteps later.

Of course, Michael had a lot of assistance from Harry Saltzman, a very powerful producer who'd already enjoyed massive success, along with Albert R. ('Cubby') Broccoli, with the James Bond films. Saltzman liked Michael, and could see his potential. He had him in mind for all the Harry Palmer movies, and helped him get his part in *Alfie* after he'd cast him in *The Ipcress File*. There was a good deal of resentment among other big names over Michael's success—though not from stars like Shelley Winters, who was the kind of person that didn't care where you came from. Quite a few major figures were unhappy when he suddenly arrived on the scene, started getting top billing, and was having scripts sent to him that they would have wanted. I think there was more jealousy on this side of the Atlantic than in America, where they like to see people get on, and would have found Mike's voice something completely new.

All stars need people they can trust, and as Mike knew he could trust me, it made sense for him to have me around. We were like brothers, really, because we got on so well together. He was aware of my background, and could be sure that I'd be able to take care of any trouble he might encounter.

Mostly, we had a good time on the sets, and he could be very generous to the people around him. In the early days, when we were about to finish a film, he'd ask me to make out a list of the cameramen and key crew members, and he'd buy them presents when he was leaving. He was generous to me, too: when I first started film work, I think I was getting something like £3 10s (£3.50) per day, but with Mike, I was earning more than £190 a week on a contract. It may not seem a lot now, but back in the 1960s, that was big money.

But it wasn't all plain sailing, and it was while we were working on *Alfie* that I first saw him blow his top. He was shooting a bedroom scene at Twickenham Studios, for which he was stripped to the waist and sitting on the edge of the bed. Somehow, a guy got onto the set and took an illicit photograph of him: it appeared in the press the next day, and Mike was understandably furious about the intrusion, and the invasion of his privacy. I don't blame him, but by then, with the photograph out there, the damage had been done.

His next picture was *The Wrong Box* (1966). It was directed by Bryan Forbes, and had a great, very English cast—Ralph Richardson, John Mills, Peter Cook and Dudley Moore, Peter Sellers, Tony Hancock, Wilfrid Lawson (he was a character!) and Bryan's wife Nanette Newman. Mike then went off to the USA to make *Gambit* (1966); I wasn't involved in it, because at that time, he wasn't really big enough to take me to the States, or to need me around him there, so I stayed in London, doing stunt work and doubling—whatever came in. But we were soon working together again on the second Harry Palmer film, *Funeral in Berlin* (1966), in which I doubled for him, and had some scary experiences while doing so.

***

Funeral in Berlin was directed by Guy Hamilton, and co-starred Oskar Homolka, Eva Renzi and Paul Hubschmid. The director of photography was Otto Heller, a little Czech guy who could be very funny. While the camera crew were shooting a scene, the clapper loader would often fetch coffee and sandwiches for them. The focus puller and camera operator would have a quick bite and a sip, put the food and drink aside to go on working...and then come back and find someone had bitten another piece out of their sandwiches. That was Otto! He'd go round, eat a bit of someone's sandwich, and put it back. He was getting on in years by this time, and there was one scene in the movie—filmed in a real underground morgue in Berlin, with actual bodies in it—that he refused to work on. He didn't like the feel of all the corpses around him, and left the job to his operator.

I didn't feature in that part of *Funeral in Berlin*, but had my own problems when I doubled for Mike in the scenes where Harry Palmer goes across to East Berlin. He couldn't appear in these himself, as we had to shoot undercover in the East, and there would have been serious trouble if we'd been caught. I was concerned for my own safety, but when I reminded the production manager that I had a wife and children, he just replied, "Don't worry: if anything happens to you, we'll send in the British Army!" I decided to go through with it, but didn't realise just how dodgy it was going to be.

Things were very tense around the Berlin Wall; in his authorised biography, *Raising Caine*, Mike has spoken about the Russians' attempts to stop us filming there by messing with our camera lenses with lights and mirrors. We had to resort to using a disguised, telescopic camera that the East Germans couldn't see, mounted in some empty buildings on the western side of the Wall. It was going to film me as I crossed into the East, and when I came back to the West after staying in East Berlin for a short time. They shouted "Action!", and as I started to make my way across, I was handed a printed notice from the American military, warning me that I'd be going over to the East at my own risk, and that they couldn't help me if anything went wrong. At that point, I couldn't turn back without ruining the shot, and I remember thinking, "I'd like to see that production manager right now!"

I was dressed up as Harry Palmer, and had his glasses on. Specs always cause difficulties for cameramen, because of problems with reflections from the lights, and we often used ones with plain glass to get round this. But my more immediate worry was that I wasn't wearing glasses in my passport photo. I walked through the 'no man's land' between the sectors, and entered the East German side, where some security ladies in green uniforms, who looked just like Gestapo officers, kept staring at me. They were very stern, miserable people, and you certainly wouldn't have wanted to upset them. One of them examined my passport, stared at me again...and pointed for me to go and stand by the wall at the back. I was held there for about ten minutes while everybody else went through the checkpoint, and I thought to myself, "This is it, I've been captured!" The guard lady then had a word with another uniformed guy—and I don't know what was said, but she and her colleague took yet another look at me, and finally waved me through.

I figured I'd had a lucky escape, and started to search for somewhere to pass the time before crossing back. All around me were deserted buildings that looked as if they'd been bombed, but when I got a bit further in, I found a sort of restaurant that was full of people, but eerily quiet: nobody at the tables seemed to be talking. It didn't feel at all right to me, but I had to wait there for about an hour, prior to making my return journey.

On the way back, I came through the checkpoint again. Just past the place where you showed your passport was a door in the corner; it led out to a wide-open space strewn with obstacles and barbed wire, beyond which was the American side. I was going through this door when I heard somebody shout out in English, "Just a minute." I kept walking, and they shouted again, so I turned round to see whether they wanted me—but in fact it was the guy behind me that they were after, and I walked straight through. When I got back, I tore into the production manager, and gave him a real mouthful because of the risks he'd exposed me to.

A few weeks later, when they'd almost finished the location shooting for the film, they decided they wanted some more shots of me in East Berlin, but I said I wasn't going over there again. In my place, they hired a young guy with a Swiss passport, and sent him across in a cab that they'd got up to look like an East German taxi. They also brought in a second unit, with a daredevil cameraman, accustomed to working in war zones, who was going to try and shoot the action from another vehicle over there.

It all went wrong when the East German cabbies spotted the fake taxi, which was quickly surrounded by guys with shooters. The driver was arrested, but the cameraman escaped. Later on, he had to abandon his 35mm movie camera in East Berlin; it had fallen out of a window from where he'd been trying to film. The Swiss boy got away with it because of his nationality, but I still think about what might have happened if it had been me, with my British passport, who'd been caught over there.

3: ON LOCATION IN THE 1960s—AND MY ROLE AS MICHAEL'S 'REGULAR MAN'

When a big film production goes on location, it's as if an entire village moves into the area chosen for the shoot. Though the producers will have arranged the whole thing, they won't be on the set every day. They may fly in now and again to see how everything's progressing, but will delegate the day-to-day work to the director, the production manager (who's in overall charge), the production secretary, and the location manager (who'll have gone out looking for the locations, and will make sure that everything's organised at them). These key people and their staff operate from an office close to the location, often in a hotel. An accountant, with an assistant, will also be working on the film from beginning to end; in fact, he'll frequently still be at work two to three months after shooting's finished, depending on the size of a production. Accountants pay out fees and salaries—not just to the actors, technicians and production staff, but to people like chauffeurs (who'll be hired locally in a foreign country), and caterers, who usually come from the UK, even when a film's being made overseas. The food they provide is eaten by the stars as well as the crew, and everyone will expect it to be tops. One of the biggest names in movie catering was a guy we called 'Swill' Hobbs, who was in charge of sourcing and supplying the meals at a string of major locations here and abroad. It's worth pointing out that all these people are only employed for the duration of the production. Once it's over, they're out of work, and their prospects of getting another job on a film depend on whether the producers like them, and decide to ask for them again. They're comparatively well-paid, but it's an insecure way to make a living.

At the shoot itself will be the cast, the crew and the production team, including three assistant directors: a first assistant, who's on the set with the director; a second assistant, who looks after the crowd and the extras; and a third assistant, who's a sort of a runabout. There are carpenters ('chippies')—some of whom are responsible for building and preparing the set, while others (the 'standbys') are there to make any last-minute changes that might be needed during shooting. And there may be additional experts and specialists, depending on the location. When we were filming out on the frozen sea in Finland for *Billion Dollar Brain* (1967: Michael Caine's co-stars were Oskar Homolka, Françoise Dorléac and Karl Malden; the director was Ken Russell), we had an 'ice doctor' who'd drill into the ice to see how thick it was, and whether it was safe for us to drive onto and set up on. There was a nurse with us too: it's always wise to have one on the set when stunts are being done, in case anybody gets hurt. I remember the *Billion Dollar Brain* nurse went wild with me when I took my hat off in the bright sunlight out in Finland (I was wearing a mink one to match Michael's, as I was doubling for him). She explained that this was potentially very dangerous, because although the sun was warm, the frozen sea obviously wasn't, and there was a risk that I'd lose so much heat from my head that I'd develop hypothermia.

I did another silly thing on that location. After a ship had been through and broken up some of the ice for us, there were big lumps of it floating around, and I started jumping from one to the other. A couple of the firemen accompanying us really had a go at me, and told me that if I'd slipped into the water, I couldn't have saved myself. It would have been impossible for my hands to get a grip on the smooth surface of the ice, and I'd have died in the sea. These firemen always carried knives, so that if they fell into the water when they were rescuing people, they could use the blades to dig into the ice and pull themselves out.

Another day when we were filming on the ice, I was going off to get Mike some tea, and saw Karl Malden standing nearby. I asked him if he'd like a cup as well. He said he'd love one, so I brought it to him...and at the end of the shoot, he came up and gave me £50! I told him I didn't want the money, but he said, "No, that was lovely of you —asking me if I wanted a cup of tea." I couldn't believe it!

The frozen conditions around Helsinki also caused problems when we were shooting on land. For one scene, we'd mounted the camera on a high platform, and I had to drive a car into the shot. I had a couple of goes to get the feel of the ice, and find out whether I'd skid.

They went all right, but when I came in on my third attempt, I lost it. The wheels jammed, and I found myself heading straight for the platform—on which the director, the camera operator, the focus puller, and three or four other technicians were all standing. I just managed to pull away in time, but it was a close thing.

All in all, I found Finland an interesting, but rather miserable place, and the low temperatures made it pretty forbidding. After a day's shooting, we used to go back to the hotel, shower and get changed, and then think about going out to get some dinner. But when we reached the front door, it was often so cold that we'd just turn round, head back inside, and eat in the restaurant on the premises instead.

Billion Dollar Brain had the biggest budget (£3 million) of all the Harry Palmer films to date, and there was so much interest in it around Helsinki that our hotel decided to lay on a big promotional evening devoted to it. They invited a hundred or so local businessmen and their wives, and asked Mike to give a speech to these people, telling them a bit about the plot and our location work. But at the last minute, he couldn't do it—he said he'd made other arrangements—and they drafted me and another actor in to take his place. I was terrified, because I'd never given a speech in my life, and I didn't want to let Mike or the local dignitaries down. I remember sitting in a room beforehand with the actor, who was as scared as I was, and downing four or five vodkas to give myself some Dutch courage. To this day, I can't recall what I said when I got in front of the guests!

I certainly wouldn't rate *Billion Dollar Brain* as one of my best locations, and I had a lot more fun in Majorca, where Mike made two films back-to-back in the late 1960s (*Deadfall*, co-starring Eric Portman, Giovanna Ralli and Nanette Newman, and directed by Bryan Forbes; and *The Magus*, co-starring Anthony Quinn and Candice Bergen, and directed by Guy Green: both were released in 1968.) We spent several months in Majorca working on *The Magus* and *Deadfall*, and started to get a bit fed up with the food there. Even the best restaurants began to lose their appeal, and Mike fancied a taste of home. There was a café where he, the crew and I used to eat quite often, and one day he said to me, "Have a word with the owner, and see if he can lay on a proper English breakfast: sausages, eggs and bacon." So I spoke to the guy, and managed to arrange it. Whenever any British press people came over to interview or photograph Mike, we'd ask them to bring sausages and other food from Harrods, and the café would cook them for us. It was a nice change from all those Spanish *chorizos*...

I got tonsillitis out in Majorca, and was off work for about a fortnight, laid up in bed at the hotel: the producers had to get me a doctor, who came to see me two or three times a week till I was cured. Another thing I won't forget about our stay on the island was shooting a scene in which I had to dive off a boat, and swim back to shore. We went for it, but as soon as I was in the water, I felt something grab me. I stopped swimming, even though the cameras were turning, and lifted up my arm to see what was going on. There was this octopus hanging off me, and I flicked it away as hard as I could. The director wasn't happy about the interruption, but I just wanted to get the thing off my arm. As soon as I'd done so, the Spanish safety guy in the boat alongside me dived in, pulled the octopus out of the water, killed it by turning it inside out, and took it home to cook it.

During one of the stunts for *Deadfall,* I was doubling for Mike in a scene where his character, Henry Clarke (who's a cat burglar) has to climb up the side of a building, and then go hand over hand in order to get into one of the rooms in the house. We were shooting in the studio, and I was about twenty feet above the ground. We did a couple of takes, but then they wanted to go for a third one—and by this time, my arms were really feeling the strain. They were hurting so much that I didn't care if I fell, even though there were no boxes or anything on the ground that could have saved me. Luckily, though, I managed to hold on, and complete the stunt safely.

Something even scarier happened after we'd finished work in Majorca, and were flying to Madrid to do a final location shoot for *Deadfall.* The night before we left, I'd had a hell of a lot to drink, and nearly missed the plane. They came and got me from my hotel, bundled me on board, and I was fast asleep throughout the flight. I didn't know until later that when we were coming into Madrid Airport at the end of the journey, the plane had nearly crashed. The location manager was there to meet us, and he saw its wing go over and touch the runway. He was about to phone London to inform them that something dreadful had happened, but the plane righted itself and landed safely. The entire production team had been on that flight, and they told me about our lucky escape afterwards. I'd been well out of it!

My daughter, Vicky, was born in 1963, and my son, Matthew in 1967. Sometimes they'd come out to the locations with Jean: Matthew was too young to join us when *The Italian Job* (1969) was being shot in Turin, though both he and Vicky came along when I was working with Mike in Malta and Africa. There was usually plenty of space to put them up. Wherever Mike went, he'd have a suite in one of the best hotels, with a large adjoining room for me; and while we were actually shooting, Jean would go off with the wife and kids of one of the producers, or with whoever Mike was seeing at the time. In the evenings, the children would go to bed, and we'd have people to keep an eye on them while we ate at the hotel's restaurant.

The Italian Job, which co-starred Noël Coward and Benny Hill, was probably one of my busiest movies. As well as playing the part of Dave (which involved whacking one of my colleagues, Dickie Graydon —see the photos), I had lots of stunt driving to do: smashing open a door for the robbers with a truck; doubling for Mike in one of the famous Mini Coopers featured in the film; and taking the place of another actor at the wheel of a Land Rover. In some of Mike's scenes, his character wasn't actually driving the car, and I never enjoyed having to be in the passenger seat for those. I don't like the feeling of not being in control of a vehicle.

I got off on the wrong foot with Peter Collinson, who directed *The Italian Job*, and had quite a short fuse. Our first meeting took place halfway up a mountain where one of the scenes was going to be shot. He travelled everywhere in a white Rolls-Royce, driven by his chauffeur, Reg, and my car happened to be blocking their path as they were coming up the road. Collinson leant out of the Rolls and shouted, "Get the f*** out of the way!" I gave as good as I got, and replied, "Who are you talking to?" I think Reg must have said to him, "That's Mike's man," and after that, Collinson and I were good friends.

Most of the stunt work for the film was done over a six-week period before the main artists came out. To make sure everything went smoothly, the producers paid out a lot of money for minders from the Mafia to keep an eye on us. If any trouble started, you could be sure they'd put a stop to it straightaway. While we were shooting the big robbery scene, there was a large crowd watching us, and just for a moment, a few guys were causing some disruption. However, one minute you saw them, and the next minute they'd gone—our Mafia friends dealt with the problem in a flash. I got to know a couple of Mafiosi: they arranged for me to visit a place where I could get a good deal on anything I wanted to buy, and came and picked me up in a car to take me there. After driving for a while, we drew up outside a house, walked straight through it—in the front and out the back—and then drove on until we reached a warehouse full of cigarettes, drink, and other goods. You name it, they had it, and I was able to get all the stuff I was after.

The stunt arranger on *The Italian Job* was a Frenchman, Rémy Julienne, who was very well-known for staging car and motor-bike accidents. He had his own team, and used a single-decker bus as a workshop, so that if anything went wrong with the stunt vehicles, they could be fixed right away. He was a lovely guy, but could be a bit nervous about things that were outside his particular area of expertise. Once, when we were about to film an explosion, I found him hiding behind a truck on the set. I asked him what he was doing, and he told me, "Oh, I don't like explosions!" "But you're supposed to be the main man here," I said; but he replied, "I do cars and motorbikes, but I never get involved in explosions."

The movie had some great stunts, and there was only one minor mishap while we were filming them. It happened when the cars were coming down the church steps during the wedding sequence. The three Mini Coopers went first, and got down OK. They were followed by a police car, which was being driven by an Italian guy—but he lost control and went skidding down the stones. Peter Collinson, who, as I've said, was very impatient, said, "Get rid of him," and ordered Reg, his own chauffeur, to "put that uniform on and drive the police car." Poor old Reg, who'd never done any stunt work or anything like that, was suddenly thrown into the front line! To film the cars coming down, they'd hidden a camera in the bushes at the bottom of the steps, and when they shouted "Action!" one of the crew would switch it on, and then go and sit on the wall just behind.

So now they're going to try and shoot the scene with Reg driving the police car. "Action!" The Mini Coopers go down, followed by Reg —but he completely loses control of his car, ploughs through the bushes where the camera's concealed, and ends up pinning the camera operator's legs to the wall he'd been sitting on. The camera guy had to be taken to hospital, but Reg wasn't hurt, though I don't think he ever got over the shock: he stuck to chauffeuring after that.

Much of *The Italian Job* was made in Turin, but we also went to Kilmainham Jail in Dublin to shoot the prison scenes featuring Noël Coward's character, Mr. Bridger. In the evenings, Mike would sometimes go out to dinner, and I'd stay in the bar at our hotel, chatting and drinking with Benny Hill, who played Professor Peach in the film. Benny was great company, and we always had a good laugh after a long day's work.

***

Looking after Mike meant travelling all over, working alongside him on most of his films, and helping him out in any way he needed. He had regular habits and routines when he was going abroad on location. He enjoyed reading, and got through books very quickly. He'd always buy a stash of the latest paperbacks from the airport bookshop before leaving, and would also take a pile of British newspapers with him; on more distant locations, these wouldn't arrive until the day after they'd been published. He and I were both music lovers, too. We'd bring along our powerful little NordMende radio-cassette machines, and Mike would have tapes of all his favourite artists: Sinatra, Barbra Streisand, Bette Midler. In those days, with no Walkmans or iPods with headphones, listening to music on the set was out of the question, so the music was strictly for Mike's leisure time...though there sometimes wasn't very much of it! I never saw him reading a book on the set, either: while he was there, he'd be totally focused on his script and his acting.

He was always highly professional—friendly with colleagues, and kind and welcoming to newcomers, whom he'd quickly put at their ease. When we began working together, he was always asking me to tell him what the various crew members did; and he already had a thorough grounding in the history of film-making, thanks to the regular visits to London's National Film Theatre he'd made at the start of his career. Having all this knowledge at his fingertips enabled him to take anything in his stride, and helped him get on well with directors, too. He was quick to build a rapport with them, even if he hadn't met them before, and was able to make light of the occasional slip-ups and problems that occur on a film set with his relaxed, humorous approach. Even on the very rare occasions when he didn't get on with a particular actor (there are a couple of examples in Chapter 4), he'd never show it, or argue with them, even when it was clear that they didn't like him.

Spending time with Mike involved quite a bit of socialising, too: Jean and I received invites to premières and fashion shows, and as a family, we were guests at Mike's mill house in Clewer Village, at Windsor, along with stars like Goldie Hawn, Sarah Miles, and Roger Moore and his then-wife Luisa. Roger and I got to be close friends: he has a great sense of humour, and on one occasion, he played a wicked, but hilarious practical joke on me when I was filming with Mike at Pinewood. I'd popped across to see what was happening on an adjacent sound stage: it was big enough to accommodate more than a hundred actors, and was being used to shoot a seafaring scene for a James Bond movie. Roger, who was on the set, caught sight of me as I slipped in to have a look, and he got hold of a microphone connected to the powerful PA system through which instructions were issued to the cast and crew. He switched it on, and I (and everyone else on the set) suddenly heard his voice booming around the vast space: "Ladies and gentlemen, it's my pleasure to tell you that we've just been joined by the great Johnny Morris!" I didn't know where to put myself!

It was Roger who recommended that Mike use some of the studio lads—painters, carpenters and what-have-you—to do a bit of building work for him at his place in Clewer. Roger had hired them previously for a project of his own, and I kept an eye on them when Mike got them in. I'd known these guys for years, but sometimes I had to crack the whip a bit: once or twice, I went down there and found them sitting by the riverbank fishing, because the house was right on the Thames. One day, I got pulled into the office by Mike's accountant, who told me the work wasn't being carried out quickly enough, and that the money being charged was getting a bit out of order. The accountant, Mike and I had a meeting, the finger was pointed at me to get rid of the studio craftsmen, and I had to tell these guys, who were old friends of mine, that they'd been fired. I don't think the construction manager ever forgave me for it, but I was acting under orders.

I was always at Mike's side—as I've said, we were like brothers—and though he had a housekeeper, a chauffeur, and one or two other staff, there was nobody else doing what I did for him. In fact, I think it may have been me who introduced him to a restaurant that became one of his favourites, the Waterside Inn at Bray, just a few miles from Clewer. The Roux brothers had opened it in 1972, and I remember dining there with Jean, my old stunting pals Terry Plummer and Mickey Ball, and their wives. Afterwards, I said to Mike, "We've had a blinding meal in a restaurant that's just around the corner from your place," and he asked me to book him a table there for eight people the next Sunday. He loved the food and the atmosphere, and quickly became a regular, along with Roger Moore, TV interviewer Michael Parkinson, and lots of other famous names.

On one occasion, I even went to Spain with Mike when he was thinking of buying a boat. A bloke at the Marbella Club, where we were staying, said that a friend of his had a big yacht that he wanted to sell. In the meantime, the bloke offered to take us out in a speedboat—a really powerful, flash one, about thirty feet long, named the *Riviera*—that belonged to another of his friends. Mike's agent, Dennis Selinger, was there too, and the three of us were given a high-speed trip along the coast, with the guy we'd met at the club taking the helm. But as we were coming past the Marbella Club on our way back, he hit a rock, tore a hole in the boat's hull, and had to switch off the engine. A load of people were watching us while sunbathing in their deck-chairs, and they seemed to find it all very exciting.

The boat was sinking fast, so we had to swim back to dry land. I told the others we should gather up our money and our watches, keep them out of the sea with one hand, and use the other hand to swim side-stroke—which we did. Suddenly, I put my foot down and found I could stand up in the water, so I shouted to Dennis Selinger, who was behind me, holding up his hand as he'd been instructed, "Come on, it's shallow here!" What I'd forgotten was that Dennis was a good bit shorter than me, so when he stood up, he sank right down and was almost totally submerged; I could just see his nose. Anyway, I pulled him up, and the four of us, soaked to the skin, made our way back to the club, with all the onlookers laughing at us. We never saw the salesman guy again...I think he left Marbella, and Mike forgot about buying boats after that.

Another part of my job was to keep everything around him running smoothly, and make sure there was no trouble—either on the movie productions themselves, or with the people who ponce around places like night clubs and restaurants, trying to make contact with the stars, and wanting to introduce people to them. Once, in Los Angeles, a bloke got into our company and said to Mike, "There's a young actress I'd like you to meet. She's a very good actress, she's very beautiful—can we have lunch?" So Mike said, "Yes, sure," and we set it up. We went along to a restaurant in LA, the guy arrived, and the girl came in and was introduced. But after a while, she decided she didn't like Mike, and started being very argumentative with him, and attacking him verbally. I could see that he was thinking, "What am I doing here?" so I told him—using back slang, which we'd both learned as kids, and would have sounded like Double Dutch to anyone else— that we should get out of there.

The next day, at about 5 o'clock in the afternoon, Mike and I were at the house in Beverly Hills he'd rented from Leslie Bricusse (who used to write songs with Anthony Newley), when all of a sudden there was a 'bang-bang-bang' at the door. It was the woman, and she was just going potty, swearing and shouting "Where is he?" She'd put her foot inside to try and stop me closing the door, so I had to push her out...and meanwhile, Mike's locked himself in his bedroom! Eventually, I told her that if she didn't leave, I'd have to call the police —because in a rich neighbourhood like that one, there are very frequent patrols, and you're likely to get picked up if you're on foot. She went away after a while, and I had to have a word with the guy who'd set up the meeting when I saw him next. I told him, "Don't ever do that again. Don't ever think of approaching Michael about introducing him to anyone else." You come across all these types, but to deal with them, all you've really got to do is use common sense. I'd seen worse situations with the people I grew up with, so I knew how to cope with that sort of thing.

There was another occasion when I told Mike we should get away from someone in LA. It was around 1968 that Mama Cass Elliot (who sang with The Mamas & The Papas) invited us to a party attended by actress Sharon Tate, hairstylist Jay Sebring, and lots of other famous names. We'd been there about a hour when Charles Manson (described as "a scruffy little man" in Mike's autobiography, *What's It*

All About?) came in, with his people. I didn't know who he was at the time, but I just didn't like it, and said to Mike, "We've got to get out of here." He asked me why, and I told him, "They're wrong'uns, we shouldn't be here." He said, "OK," and we left. Not long afterwards, Sharon Tate and Jay Sebring were killed by the so-called Manson Family, and Manson himself is still serving a life sentence for murder and conspiracy—so, as Mike has said, it was a good job he listened to me. He was aware of my background, knew that I'd known some of the big heavies in London, and realised it'd be wise to heed my advice.

Sometimes, it could be fun to meet figures from the American underworld. In March 1971, while we were in New York to see the Joe Frazier-Muhammad Ali boxing match at Madison Square Garden, we were introduced to a character called Little Benny, a dapper little guy who, we were told, "ran the Puerto Ricans" in the city. He dressed very much like an Englishman—collar and tie, sports jacket—and he arranged to pick us up one night and show us his clubs. We drove off with him in his big limousine, and at the second venue we visited, we met the biggest, tallest, fattest lady I'd ever seen. She ran the club, and when you were introduced to her, she got hold of you, put her arms around you, and tilted backwards so that your feet came off the ground! Everywhere we went with Little Benny, there was a second guy always sitting at a table behind us. Little Benny saw that I'd noticed him, and said, "John, don't worry about him: he's with me." Benny told me that he'd have loved to go to England, but knew they wouldn't allow him in, and said, "Next time you're in New York, let me know. I've got a place upstate where you can hide out, and you can stay there whenever you like."

Mike had his own way of 'hiding out,' or, at any rate, taking an occasional break from the pressures of fame. A couple of times, in New York and LA, he just disappeared for a few hours—and it turned out that he'd gone to see a movie on his own. When it happened in New York, I was so worried that I rang someone with what you might call 'connections,' who told me, "If he isn't back by a certain time, we'll send out the troops." (I think he meant 'the heavy mob'!) But thankfully, Mike showed up at the hotel an hour later, and said he'd simply fallen asleep in the cinema. In LA, he left a movie house, started to walk back to the villa we'd rented, and got pulled up by the police, who, as I've explained, are always very suspicious of anyone walking around at night in that part of Beverly Hills. When they asked him who he was, and he replied, "My name is Michael Caine," they didn't believe him. "OK, buddy," they said, "get in the patrol car"...but once they took him to the police station, they realised he was telling the truth. He stuck around chatting to them for two or three hours, before they gave him a lift back home.

Mostly, though, Mike would rest and relax in the company of other big stars. On one occasion, he and I were invited out to dinner by Elizabeth Taylor, who was in Los Angeles at the same time as us. Elizabeth was with Richard Burton at the time, and they were staying in a villa at the Beverly Hills Hotel (a long-time favourite of theirs) where we met up before the meal. When we arrived, she introduced us to a so-called 'producer,' who, I found out later, was really just a 'hanger-on.' He'd had a few drinks, and was boasting about being able to set Elizabeth up in some sort of film project. His behaviour was upsetting everybody, so she asked me to get rid of him. Once I'd shown the guy the door, which I was able to do without any difficulty, the four of us went out for a meal together.

Another time in LA, things weren't quite so peaceable. We'd been visiting a couple of nightclubs: one of them, the *Daisy*, was a favourite of Frank Sinatra's, and Sinatra happened to be in the club while Mike and our party were there; he and his people were sitting at a table near us. A friend of mine who lived in the city was dancing with a girl at the club that evening, when a guy he didn't know came up and touched him on the shoulder, as if the dance was an 'excuse-me'...Afterwards, I wound my mate up about it. "What's that all about?" I asked. "This is a nightclub, and people don't come up and touch you on the shoulder like that. The guy's having a go at you!" "I think you're right," he said, and he went over to the guy who'd tried to break up his dance and chinned him!

It all started then. Because I'd wound my friend up, I felt I had to go over and help him, and they finished up having to carry out the guy who'd caused all the trouble. Sinatra was watching all this going on from his table. And I'll never forget: as he left with his people, he came over to us and said, "I love you Limeys!"

My father, 'Gentleman Jim' Morris (on the left) with my Uncle Arthur, who was a famous light heavyweight boxer.

An old photo of my father and one of my many half-brothers, James Jnr.

EARLS COURT EXHIBITION 1893
CAPTAIN PAUL BOYTON'S WATER SHOW
ARTHUR MORRIS (Fulham) and ALBERT PEARCE (American Coloured Champion)
Daily Exhibition Boxing Displays

Arthur Morris
Born 10ᵗʰ September, 1873.
Beechill, Walton Abbey.

Paddington Baths

Promoter of many boxing shows at Wonderland, Chelmsford,
Hounslow, Ealing, Esccourt School of Arms and Kew.
1892 to 1902

Open Air Picture Palace

ARTHUR MORRIS beat ALLINGHAM (Isle of Wight) same year for £100 aside for Captain Beckett and afterwards met such men as
DIDO PLUMB at Riley's Hotel Newmarket for £160 aside, FRANK CRAIG (The Coffee Cooler) America at the Central Hall Holborn,
TED BRYANT at Lambeth School of Arms £25 aside £75 purse, MYSTERIOUS BILLY SMITH (America) at Tottenham, STARLIGHT
THE BLACK (Australia) at Royal Aquarium, NED RYAN (Limerick) at Bob Habbijam's, Newman Street TED FENTON at Kennington
Social Club, TED RICH at the Bolingbroke Club, BEN TAYLOR (Woolwich), GUNNER MOIR (Lambeth), ARTHUR MORRIS also met
KIT MARNEY (Deptford) in a 4 round trial for purse at National Sporting Club on the night of the Kohnny O'Brien v David St John (Wales)
Fight. He also appeared in the great "Derby Scene" and other big boxing displays at Olympia.
ARTHUR MORRIS also met the CHAMPION OF THE WORLD JAMES J. JEFFRIES at the Royal Aquarium in 1899, and afterwards
Boxed with allcomers for months nightly, also gave exhibition boxing at all the principal halls in London with all the different champions

An illustrated card from my archive, giving details of my Uncle Arthur's impressive boxing career.

A damaged picture fragment showing my father (on the left) and another man boxing blindfolded. Nearly all the onlookers are in uniform, and mock sporting contests like this were popular with soldiers during World War I.

The passing-out parade after my National Service basic training. I'm the second soldier from the right in the front row, and we're being inspected by the Catholic padre, Fr. Williams.

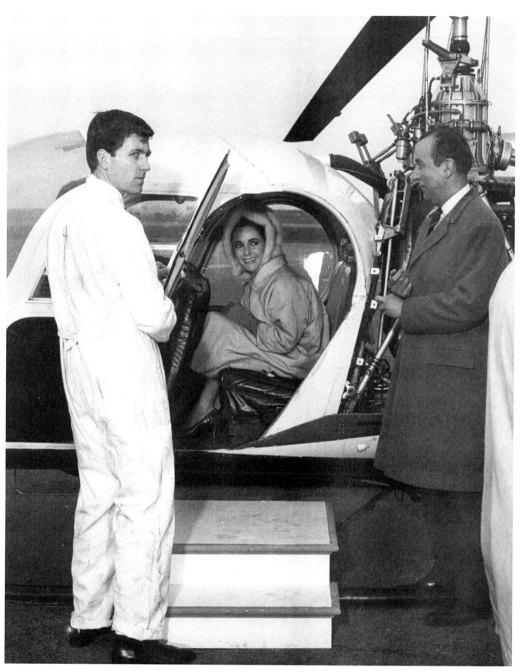

I'm on the left in the next two pictures, assisting Elizabeth Taylor as she leaves a helicopter in *The V.I.P.s* (1963); on the right is Dennis Price. Elizabeth's co-stars in the movie included Richard Burton, Orson Welles, Margaret Rutherford and Maggie Smith. The director was Anthony Asquith.

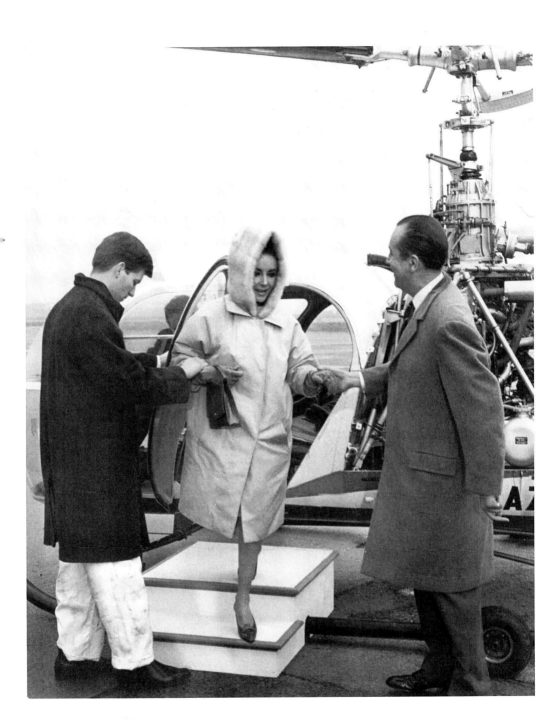

The next few pages feature some of my own photos, taken in May 1965 on the set of the second Beatles movie, *Help!*; they've never been published before. The location is Cliveden House, near Maidenhead. Here, Paul McCartney (with a baseball and glove) is surrounded by a group of actors and crew. The smiling guy next to him is Eddie Dillon, Ringo Starr's stand-in.

George Harrison, John Lennon and Paul McCartney on the terrace at Cliveden House, talking to Walter Shenson, the producer of *Help!*

I was John Lennon's stand-in on *Help!* and *A Hard Day's Night*: here I am with Ringo, George and John.

You can see me more clearly in this side view, with Ringo on my left.

George, John, and Eddie Dillon.

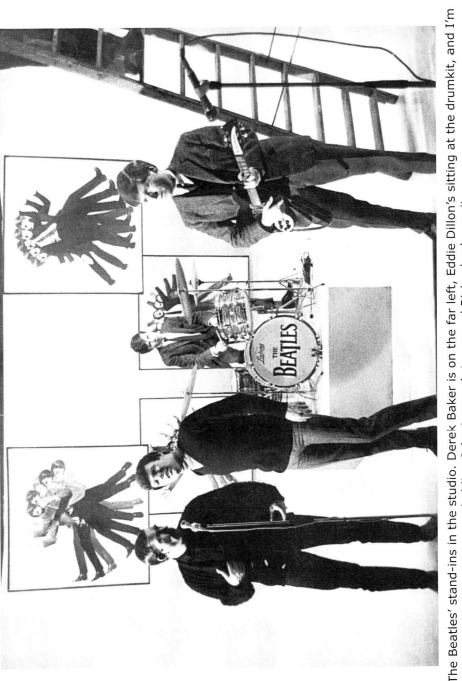

The Beatles' stand-ins in the studio. Derek Baker is on the far left, Eddie Dillon's sitting at the drumkit, and I'm holding John Lennon's treasured Rickenbacker guitar.

Taking a rest at Cliveden during the *Help!* shoot. Beside the publicity lady are Ringo and George; the man with the airline bag is actor Victor Spinetti.

Here, we're setting up a scene for *Help!* in a field. I'm standing in the foreground with my hands in my pockets. I wonder what the director, Dick Lester (on the ground) is saying to John Lennon, whose distinctive cap is just visible down the hole?

Shooting a scene for *The Ipcress File*. I'm at the wheel of the Merc, and Bill Sulley ('Smuggler Bill') is the gunman on the right of the picture.

In Hyde Park with Michael Caine while we were making *The Ipcress File*. Mike wrote the following message on the back of the photo: "So far John you've been marvellous and I'm sure you always will be, let's hope we can stay together."

I took this photo of Michael through a screen on the set of *The Ipcress File*.

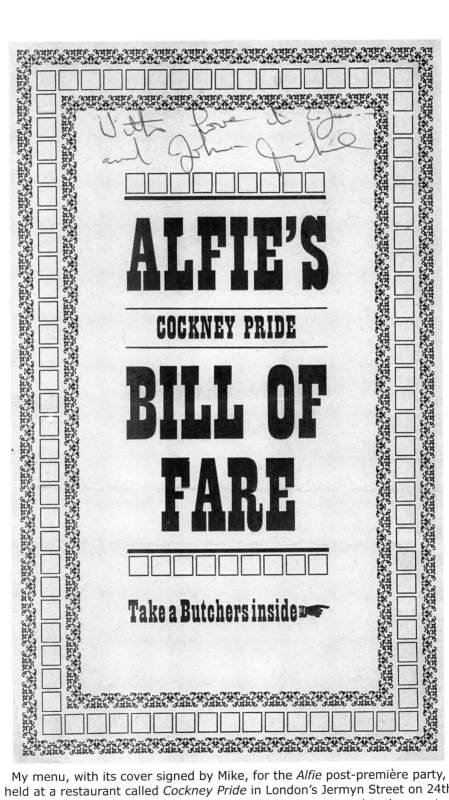

ALFIE'S

COCKNEY PRIDE

BILL OF FARE

Take a Butchers inside 👉

My menu, with its cover signed by Mike, for the *Alfie* post-première party, held at a restaurant called *Cockney Pride* in London's Jermyn Street on 24th March 1966. The following two pages show what was served to the guests.

VICTUALS

Savelloys and Pease Pudding

Shepherd's Pie

Steak & Kidney Pie
with mashed potatoes

Salmon Fishcakes
with mashed potatoes

Oxtail with Buttered Beans
and mashed potatoes

Faggots and Pease Pudding

Australian Mutton Pie

Boiled Beef and Carrots

Curried Beef

and

Bangers served with a choice of
mashed or bubble and squeak

Aunt Mary's Apple Pie

Rice Pudding

PLEASE DO NOT SPIT ON THE FLOOR

For the Toffs who haven't got the courage...

Fresh Salmon and

Smoked Salmon

and

Sundry delicacies

on the cold

buffet

**PLEASE ORDER FROM THE BAR
OR THE WAITRESSES
ANY ALCOHOLIC BEVERAGES
THAT YOU MAY DESIRE**

On location for *Funeral in Berlin*. I'm doubling for Mike as Harry Palmer, and getting ready to cross into the East. Those glasses nearly got me into trouble at the checkpoint!

On the frozen Finnish sea with Mike while we were making *Billion Dollar Brain*. I'm on the left.

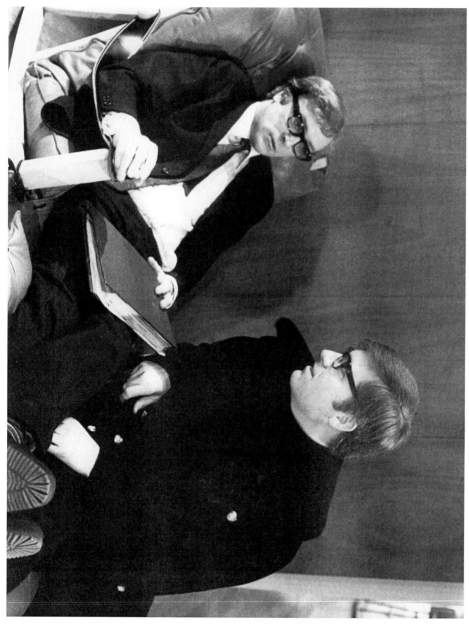

A more comfortable studio shot from *Billion Dollar Brain.*

On location for *Deadfall* in Majorca, with Mike's co-star Giovanna Ralli.

L–R: Roy Pontin (wardrobe), Freddie Williamson (make-up), Michael Caine and me, photographed in Majorca during work on *Deadfall*.

CALL SHEET

SALAMANDER FILM PRODUCTIONS LTD.   No. 94 (STUDIO)

PRODUCTION NAME :- "DEADFALL"	PROD. No. :- SFP/107

STAFF CALL :- 6.30 P.M. (ELECTRICAL & CONSTRUCTION)   CALL FOR DATE :- TUESDAY/WEDNESDAY
7.00 P.M. (REMAINDER UNIT)   12/13 SEPT 1967

SETS OR LOCATIONS :-   EXT. GARDENS OF LAGRANJA'S HOUSE   STUDIO GARDENS

ARTISTES	DRESSING ROOM No.	CHARACTER	TIME REQUIRED AT STUDIO	TIME REQUIRED ON SET
MICHAEL CAINE	90 F.	HENRY	8.00 pm	8.30 pm
STAND-IN: JOHN MORRIS	"	For Mr. Caine	7.00 pm at Studio.	

PROPS: To include: Safe, Chunks of meat, Henry's Tool Kit, Rope
                Plus: Two Alsations c/o Bowesmoor Kennels, at Studio 7.00pm

OTHER REQUIREMENTS:

MEDICAL: First Aid Man (with Kit) to be in attendance from 6.30 pm.

ELECTRICAL/
CONSTRUCTION.   3 Lighting Towers required.

TELEPHONE: 2 Night Lines to be open: Unit Office - Iver 717 (Room 39 C Block)
                                           Mr. Bryan Forbes' Dressing Room Iver 715.
                                                                    (Room 89 F Block)

CATERING: BUFFET: 8.00 - 9.30 pm.   )
                MEAL BREAK: 11.30pm - 12.30 am) For approximately
                TEA & SANDWICHES: 2.00 - 3.00 am   ) 80 persons.
                BREAKFAST:)
                available from   4.30 am   )

RUSHES: THEATRE 1 - 7.00 p.m.

TRANSPORT: (1) Car to pick up Mr. Caine as arranged.
                (2) Coach to be at 'White Horse' Public House, Belmont Road, Uxbridge
                    at 6.15 pm and return 6.45 pm for conveyance to Studio.
                    NOTE - Coach to stand by from 5.00 am Wednesday morning at
                    Time Keepers Gate for conveyance of Unit to Uxbridge.

SCENE NUMBERS :-   200, 208, 357, 363, 367, 371, 374, 376, 379, 382, 386, 393 NIGHT

ASSISTANT DIRECTOR
CHRISTOPHER DRYHURST

A call sheet, like this one for *Deadfall,* is drawn up for every day of a movie shoot. It tells actors and crew when and where they'll be required, and provides other essential information—including details of meal times!

"Dave, get rid of that water carrier!" Dickie Graydon (right) doing a stunt with me for *The Italian Job*.

Preparing for another *Italian Job* stunt: I'm at the wheel of a truck that's about to be used to ram a door.

I'm on the left, standing in a Turin street during work on *The Italian Job*.

Model Bianca Macias (Mike's then-girlfriend, later to become Bianca Jagger) visits the *Italian Job* set. Mike's in the centre, and I'm on the left. On the far right are two electricians whose careers—like mine—began when they worked for the Lee brothers, rigging lights for exhibitions at Earls Court and Olympia.

The robbery gang from *The Italian Job*, disguised as football supporters. Coco, played by Michael Caine's brother Stanley, is second from left; I'm on the far right.

4: WORKING WITH MICHAEL AT HOME AND ABROAD

Once Michael became a big name, he was appearing in a considerable number of films: two, and sometimes three a year. He used to say that he'd take on everything, because he wanted to get lots of money...and he did make some bad pictures along with the great ones! Working for him, and being constantly on call, meant that I no longer needed to seek out temporary jobs between movie projects. Previously, I'd chauffeured for Rolls-Royce in South Kensington, taking clients to air shows and Ascot races—but by 1967, I was able to buy a Rolls for myself, and when I saw one advertised, I went down to the seller's home in Maidenhead with my friend Michael Douglas, who'd worked for me as a stunt man on several movies, to check it out. The car I was interested in was a 1958 Silver Cloud I, with midnight blue paintwork and white upholstery. But when the guy in Maidenhead opened the door of his double garage, we were amazed to see a pair of Rolls-Royces, both exactly the same colour. Mike Douglas and I looked at each other: he was pretty shrewd, and wondered whether there might be something dodgy about the two very similar cars. However, they turned out to be entirely genuine: one was a slightly later model (a Silver Cloud III), but I was interested in the SI, and I decided to buy it on the spot, paying cash. It was such a beautiful car, and I drove it for nine years.

Earlier on, when I'd needed the work, I'd also done modelling assignments—and one of the best of them was a two-week stint in Majorca with Miss South Africa. I'd been hired by a stills photographer I knew, and we went all around the island, shooting different scenes. While I was posing in the sea there, I trod on a sea urchin. Their spines pierce your skin and cause a lot of pain, and I had to come out of the water and get my foot treated, which upset the shoot. Miss South Africa—who, I recall, wasn't a very friendly lady—

wasn't too pleased, but the job was certainly a good one.

I didn't have as much fun when I was hired to be one of the flunkies for the Miss World contest at the Lyceum in London in 1963. When I got there for the rehearsals on the first day, I found that all the girls, and Eric Morley, the organiser, were already on stage with my fellow flunky, so I took a seat in the audience area beside some of the technical people and hangers-on, hoping I wouldn't be noticed. All of a sudden, Morley called out, "Where's the other flunky?" I didn't want him to see I was sitting there, and was beginning to think that I didn't really fancy the job in any case, so I stayed still and kept watching. About ten minutes went by, and Morley shouted out again, "Where's this effing flunky?" I decided I'd better dive round, and make it look as though I'd just arrived. After doing that, I apologised to Morley for being late, but he gave me a right coating in front of everybody. The next day, I got fitted out with all the flunky gear...and I somehow managed to stay the course for the four days I was booked for. Over the years, my other temporary work included selling double-glazing (it was made from aluminium in those days—they weren't using plastic yet); and a good bit later, I looked after a seven-year-old Arab prince who was staying in a penthouse suite at the Dorchester with his royal parents. I got that job through a couple of ex-Army guys I knew, who ran a company providing security and bodyguards. I'd take the boy shopping in the West End, and we'd visit the Zoo and sometimes go to Hyde Park.

In the late 1960s, though, I was fully occupied with my film career, not only as Mike's double and stunt man, but also as a stunt arranger —working out the most effective way to stage fights, falls, and action shots, and employing people to do them. My first stunt arranging job was for *Play Dirty*, which was shot in Spain, co-starred Nigel Davenport and Nigel Green, and was released in 1969. Another movie, *Shalako* (1968), featuring Sean Connery and Brigitte Bardot, was being made out there at the same time. In his autobiography, Mike describes our first meeting with Brigitte in Spain, and how she gave us a ride in her white Rolls-Royce, together with her glamorous employees Gloria and Monique—two ladies (nicknamed Glo Glo and Mo Mo) who, as Mike says, were "almost as attractive" as their famous boss. I met Bardot again a few weeks later, at a surprise birthday party Mike had arranged for me at a local restaurant. I was sitting at a table there, surrounded by friends, when two hands reached over from behind me and covered my eyes. I turned round, saw Brigitte—whom Mike had invited as well, unbeknown to me—and received a kiss on the cheek from her as a birthday gift.

Because the production schedules for the two movies were overlapping, I thought I'd try to 'borrow' a stunt girl from *Shalako*—Dorothy Ford, an old friend, who'd just completed her work on that picture—for *Play Dirty*. But Bob Simmons, who was in charge of the *Shalako* stunting, got annoyed about it, and sent someone over to ask me what I thought I was up to, trying to "nick his staff." Actually, my asking for Dorothy wasn't so unusual, as I'd been 'borrowed' for a stunt myself a couple of years earlier, while I was working on *Funeral in Berlin*. Another film unit was shooting *The Quiller Memorandum* (1966) in the city: its stunt arranger wanted me to double for George Segal (who took the title role) in a car crash scene that was being shot at night, and I'd had no problem getting permission from my producers to do it. But even though Dorothy had finished stunting on the Sean Connery film, I couldn't get her for *Play Dirty*, so I arranged for another friend, Sadie Eden, to come out from England and work with me.

I was also a close friend of Sadie's husband, a stunt man who'd just been released from prison. His nickname was 'Blow-Up Eddie,' because after he'd found out that Sadie was having an affair, he'd tried to blow her lover up by attaching explosives to the underside of his car! Someone spotted him planting them, and he got arrested and jailed. He needed work after completing his five-year sentence, and I was able to get him a stunting job on the picture too. He wasn't keen to leave Sadie on her own, so it suited him to accompany her to Spain.

Some of the stunts on *Play Dirty* were pretty rough. One of them was a fight between me and Sadie (who was stunt doubling for actress Vivian Pickles) that started in the back of an army ambulance. Sadie had to kick me off the vehicle—it was a two-foot drop onto the ground —jump out after me, get hold of me again, and flip me over as we were lying on the sand. While we were shooting the scene, I did a somersault and went down...but I hadn't checked the place where I was going to land, which turned out to have hard rock just underneath its sandy surface. The rock gave me a nasty whack on the back of my neck, and though I didn't think much about it at the time, it's caused me some problems since. On another stunt, I was lying face-down, looking over some cliffs, and the director, André de Toth, took Sadie's place in order to demonstrate what he wanted her to do to me while I was on the ground. He was as strong as an ox, and when he climbed onto me and pulled my head back by grabbing hold of my hair, I suddenly felt blood trickling down my forehead: he'd pulled some of the hair up by its roots! That was André—an absolute nutter. There was an even more dangerous scene in the movie, where a truck is tumbling down a mountain slope with all its contents falling out, and Mike's character runs down after it to try and save it. Obviously, I was doubling for him here, and having to jump around on the mountainside like a kangaroo, so as to avoid getting hit by all the stuff from the truck! Luckily, I didn't fall over, and we succeeded in filming the whole stunt in a single take.

As you can imagine, seeking out the locations needed for a film like this was quite a challenge, and while doing so, Ray Freeborn, the location manager, had an unpleasant experience that became a big joke among his colleagues. He'd been checking out a cave for a particular scene; it was occupied by a group of gypsies, and after going in to see if it was any good for shooting, he found he couldn't stop scratching himself—as he was smothered in fleas! Poor old Ray...

Play Dirty's director, André de Toth, had originally been the movie's associate producer, but was promoted by the producer, Harry Saltzman, after the first director was sacked. As I mentioned in Chapter 2, Harry had spotted Michael Caine's potential early on. He was a very hard man, but of all the many producers I worked for, I think he was my favourite—and if he took a liking to you, he was always loyal and friendly. He'd invite Mike and his girlfriends, and me and my family, over to his house for lunch and for weekends; and while we were working on *Play Dirty* in Spain, he'd sometimes take a group of about ten of us out to dinner. He was very particular about the places we ate, though. He'd inspect the kitchens of any restaurants we visited, and if he didn't like what he saw, he'd say, "Come on, we're not staying here!" and we'd go somewhere else.

Harry Saltzman would always be the first person on the set in the morning, and people knew they had to arrive in good time, because he'd be there waiting. And he'd never stand any nonsense from actors, however famous they were. Richard Harris had originally been cast alongside Mike in *Play Dirty*, but the two of them didn't get on. For the first few days of the shoot, Harris would arrive at the location in the Almería desert, go to his caravan, get made up, and then refuse to appear on set...all because Mike had the bigger part. Eventually, Harry lost patience with Richard, and sacked him from the film. Several years later, there was still bad blood between the two actors as a consequence of this. One evening in the early 1970s, when we were in Malta, we found ourselves in the same restaurant as Richard, who was with his songwriter, Jimmy Webb, and had had a few drinks. Things started to get nasty, with Richard shouting across the room to Mike, and Mike shouting back to him. A couple sitting at a table in between us called for the manager and said, "This is ridiculous. We came in here to eat, not listen to two people shouting at one another." I knew what Richard was like, and had to get up and smooth it all out. If things had gone any further, and Mike had said something wrong, I reckon Richard would have come over, and there would have been trouble.

Because I was so close to Mike, I could tell when things were worrying him. I think he got lonely sometimes: he had a lot of weight on his shoulders, especially when he was the main lead in a film. He was also uneasy if he was up against actors who'd been in the business longer than him...which was the situation on *Battle of Britain* (1969), his next film after *Play Dirty*. Among the many other stars in that cast were Laurence Olivier (Mike was very conscious of Olivier's status and reputation, and his ability to steal a scene), Ralph Richardson, Michael Redgrave and Trevor Howard. The director was Guy Hamilton. In fact, Mike and I were only on the *Battle of Britain* set for a short time, and I don't think Mike enjoyed doing the picture at all. I remember him saying to me on his last day of shooting, "Go and get the car, John, let's get out of here." He hadn't ever done that before.

He was much happier while making *Too Late The Hero* (1970), for which he had six weeks of rehearsals in Los Angeles, before going off to the Philippines on location. This was probably because he was working with lots of British actors he knew: Ronnie Fraser, Percy Herbert, Lance Percival—all fun guys. The director, Bob Aldrich (who also directed *The Dirty Dozen*) was a friendly Anglophile with a passion for fitness; and though he was nicknamed 'Butterball,' and possessed what Mike's biographer, William Hall, describes as a "formidable physical girth," he was always in shorts, had muscles on his legs that were like footballs, and used to travel with a personal masseur. We spent lots of time at his house in LA, which was like an English mansion, and were also invited to brunch by Bill Cosby, who lived nearby. There were quite a few famous fellow-guests there, including Doris Day, one of my favourite singers and actresses—I couldn't believe I was sitting next to her! Cosby, like Bob Aldrich, had a pool table at his home, and after the meal, one of his friends challenged us to a game. Because I'd spent half my life in snooker halls around Shepherd's Bush and Hammersmith, adapting to pool was easy for me, and I finished up beating everyone I took on at it in LA. The Americans were good players, and couldn't understand how I was able to thrash them, but I wasn't even trying: I was just potting balls in my usual way, and they were going in!

The main purpose of the LA rehearsals for *Too Late The Hero* was to work on the dialogue with the actors, who mostly sat round a table going through it with Aldrich. There were quite a few ensemble scenes, so the process was essential—though it didn't bring Mike any closer to the one member of the cast he had problems with, Cliff Robertson. Even when they were actually shooting the film, the two of them just didn't connect. Often, when Mike came off a set, he'd ask me, "How was that? What did you think of it?" But after finishing a scene with Robertson, he said, "I can't make him out. When I'm talking to him, he won't look at me. He keeps looking away. What do you think it is?" I answered: "Well, you're the main billing, and he's not, though he's better known than you. Maybe that's upset him."

Arranging food and accommodation for the cast and crew out in the Philippines took some doing. The US Navy's Subic Bay naval base was nearby, and Bob Aldrich, Mike and I, the other actors, and the cameramen were given special permission to eat in its sergeants' mess every evening. I got into a bit of trouble when I first showed up there. All the servicemen at the tables around us had very short haircuts, as did Mike and the actors, but I had longer hair, and wanted to hang onto it. When the Americans saw me, they weren't happy, and said, "You've got to have your hair cut." When I asked why, they just told me I was "causing a problem;" I suppose it was all to do with military discipline. Anyway, I reluctantly got it cut, but it worked out OK for me, as I ended up being given a small part in the film that needed short hair.

We couldn't actually live at the naval base, and the lodgings Aldrich found for us were rather unusual; he'd come across them earlier, while looking for places where he could shoot. A local madam was building a brothel in the area; she'd run out of money, and only its ground floor had been constructed. Aldrich said to her, "If I give you the cash to get it finished, can we stay there?" She agreed, he gave her the funds she needed to complete the place, and we all lived in it while the movie was being made. After we'd gone, she was in business! The rooms weren't too bad, and there was a lovely swimming pool in the grounds, but none of us wanted to use it, because the water in it had turned a murky colour in the heat—I don't think it was being looked after properly. Security was also a problem: we had armed guards to keep an eye on the cameras and equipment stores, but some stuff still went missing, even though we never got robbed ourselves.

For one of the actors, Percy Herbert (cast as Sergeant Johnstone), making *Too Late The Hero* must have stirred up terrible memories. In real life, he'd been a prisoner of war in Changi during World War II, and he had to be kept away from the Japanese cast on the set, or he'd have torn into them. And day-to-day conditions on the set could be pretty gruelling for the other actors and crew as well. Every morning, before we began shooting, a guy would walk through the undergrowth in front of us with a stick, beating the ground and making a noise. Mike told me this was being done in order to get rid of any animals—snakes, or whatever—that might be in our path. "What happens if one's deaf?" I asked him. "We're in trouble then, aren't we?" One day, I was on a beautiful, deserted beach at the edge of the jungle when I saw Ian Bannen (who played Private Thornton in the film) come wandering out of the rainforest clutching his script, with a copy of the Bible inside it. He was delirious—he'd got heatstroke or something, and didn't know what he was doing—and just kept walking straight towards the sea. I had to get hold of him and help him back to the shore. Another actor refused to eat the food on location, which was being provided by local caterers, and wasn't very good. He lived on paw-paw fruit instead, and it made his face swell up, so that he only had slits for his eyes. They had to bring in a doctor for him, as he was in a terrible state, and we couldn't shoot with him until he'd got back to normal. When something unexpected like that happens, a good production manager is worth his or her weight in gold, as they'll have contingency plans to ensure that work on the film can still go ahead, even if a cast member goes sick for a few days.

I had a nasty health scare myself in the Philippines, after something bit me on the leg while I was in bed. I never found out what did it, though it may have been a spider; but the bite was very painful, and swelled up so much I could hardly walk. They sent me to the American hospital at Subic Bay for treatment, but I took about two weeks to get better, and still have a mark on my leg. After that, I was always anxious about the conditions in my sleeping quarters, and I remember being especially unhappy with the temporary accommodation that had been provided for me and Michael while we were shooting in the jungle. They'd given us a horrible little room with two single beds—hot and humid, and in the densest part of the forest—and I decided to give it a thorough spray with some pesticide before we went out, closing the door and windows tightly behind us. When we came back, there were about eight lizards on the floor in there, lying on their backs with their legs up in the air. The spray had killed them, and some of the crew were winding me up about it —"Look what you've done!"—but I told them, "There's no way I'm going to get bitten again." It's an odd thing, though: when you first go into the jungle, your nerves are on edge all the time, because there's bush all around you, and you don't know what's going to come out at you, or what may be hanging from the branches. But after a while, the humidity gets to you, and you just stop caring what happens.

Despite the hardships, we had a lot of fun in the Philippines. We were on especially good terms with our American crew, and were always trying to outdo each other with our practical jokes. In one hotel we were staying in, there was a giant seashell that was being used as an oversized ashtray. I got one of our guys to help me carry it upstairs and put it into an American crew member's bed. We covered it up, and waited for the bloke to turn in that night. He opened his bedroom door, saw this mysterious shape under the sheet, and screamed out, "What's going on? There's some sort of animal in my bed!" Then he went downstairs to fetch the hotel's management, because he didn't know what was in there. When they came up and saw the shell, they had a good laugh...and we did too, because we were just waiting for him to react like that. The Americans had their revenge on us a couple of weeks later. They got hold of a dead snake — I think it was a really big water snake, about three and a half feet long —and put it in my bed. I didn't see it until I pulled back the sheet, and it frightened the life out of me: I went running out of that room, and they were round the corner laughing their heads off!

While we were shooting the film, we used to work in the jungle for about fourteen days straight, then have four days off. At the start of these breaks, an old Dakota aircraft whose regular cargo was fish (and which always stank of it!) would take us to Manila. From there, we could travel on to Hong Kong, Taiwan, or wherever Mike and the other stars wanted to go. At the end of the rest period, we'd return to Manila to be flown back to the movie location in the Dakota. One day, just after take-off, its main door suddenly came open at the back, and everyone was asked to interlock their arms in a chain so that Cliff Robertson—an experienced aviator, who was at the end of the line— could lean out and close it while we held onto him. That was the kind of flight (and the kind of dirty, stinking, rotten plane) you don't forget in a hurry!

The biggest urban centre near the location was Olongapo City. One evening, a security guy from the American base asked if Mike and I would like to see the sights down there. We met him at his house, and just before he drove us into town, I saw him strap his gun on. He clearly wasn't taking any chances, even though he was a well-known figure in the area, and when he took us onto the main street in Olongapo we could understand why. It was like a sort of Wild West town, full of nightclubs, bars, gambling and prostitution, where some of the American servicemen at Subic Bay used to go for a night out after fighting in Vietnam. They'd be letting off steam, drinking and firing guns, but nobody—not even the military patrols—would interfere with them, and the local police just let them have their head, because everyone knew that these guys might be going off to get killed in the war the next day.

Mike and I also visited the military hospital where wounded US personnel were being treated. We saw a guy there covered in bandages, with only his mouth, nose and eyes visible. I asked one of the nurses what had happened to him; I assumed he'd been injured in the war, but she told me he'd been attacked in the town—robbed and cut with knives by the local thugs. When the Yanks were returning from Olongapo, they'd often be blind drunk and all over the place, which made them easy targets for the bandits. To get back into the base, they had to cross a bridge spanning a filthy stream, and the robbers would snatch their watches and wallets, and drop them over the bridge into the dirty water, where there were kids waiting to grab whatever was thrown to them. Everyone wore short-sleeved shirts in the intense heat, and we were warned never to leave our watches on, as they were so easy to tear off our wrists. Even the roads around Olangapo could be hair-raising, especially at night, when animals would often get caught in our headlights, and run over. The most gruesome bit of roadkill I saw was a massive, thick-bodied snake, lying all crushed up on the side of the highway.

An officer once invited us on board an American aircraft carrier at Subic Bay: we were given cigarette lighters from the mess as souvenirs of our visit, and they laid on a demonstration of how their aircrew could be rescued if they got shot down in the jungle. Every pilot carried an attachment that released a balloon on a cable, and a plane would see it, fly over, and use a sort of fork to grab the cable and winch the pilot up. After we'd been shown it in action, they asked me if I wanted a go—but I said, "Not at the moment, thank you!"

It was my idea to organise something called the 'Olongapoo Patrol' (we spelt the place's name with a double 'o' at the end). This was a group of actors and other film people that we set up so we could look out for each other in the town, and make sure none of us got into trouble with gambling or any of the other temptations on offer there. When we were thinking about a night out, we'd say, "Right, where's the Olongapoo Patrol?" We even had a signed certificate of membership, and you can see a picture of it in the photo section.

Soon after we'd finished *Too Late The Hero*, Mike and I went to Austria, where we were on location for *The Last Valley* (1970). The scriptwriter and director was James Clavell (also a best-selling novelist, and the author of *The Great Escape's* award-winning screenplay), and the film co-starred Omar Sharif. In one of his books, Mike recalls a stormy incident that occurred during the shooting of the movie—and it's something that I'm unlikely to forget, either. It happened in the bar at a hotel in Innsbruck where we were staying. Mike, his then-girlfriend Minda Feliciano (whom he'd met in the Philippines), Omar Sharif and I had a regular spot there: a table with a long bench near the entrance. One evening, a female member of the cast was sitting at the bar, a few feet away from us, having a drink; and next to her was a group of about twelve Greek students, who'd come in because they'd found out we were filming in the area. I don't think they meant any harm at first, but one of them, a sort of ringleader, decided to try it on with the actress. He said something to her, and knocked the cigarette she was smoking out of her hand. It flew over, and, of all the people it could have fallen onto, it landed on Minda—dropped more-or-less straight into her lap.

Doing that was like throwing a firework. Minda called out, "John!" Mike looked at me too, and straightaway I got up, grabbed hold of the guy who'd caused the problem, and pushed him out into the lobby. The next thing I knew, the hotel manager had been called, and was talking to the guy—but I reached over the top of the manager's back and gave the student a dig. Then it really started, with fights breaking out everywhere, and all the students getting involved...just like a movie set! I can still remember one of the actors in the bar—Chris Chittell, who played Svenson in the film, and is now famous as Eric Pollard in *Emmerdale*—saying, "I'm with you, John!" and helping me out. He was a very fit guy, and he rushed one of the Greek students, got him in a headlock, and crashed through two swing doors with him. Just around the corner, a couple of the stunt boys from the film —Rocky Taylor and Terry Plummer—were playing cards, and while I was fighting with one or two of these Greeks, I looked over to see what Terry Plummer, in particular, was going to do. He was a real handful, a massive guy who'd once been a minder for some North London villains (the Nash brothers), and was frightened of no one. He never went out looking for trouble, and you'd have to hit him over the head with an iron bar to start him off—but once he did lose it, you had to get out of the way. To my surprise, he just stood and watched what was going on. Afterwards I said to him, "Terry, I looked like getting my head kicked in there. Why didn't you help me out?" He replied, "No...I could see you was doing alright!"

Anyway, now all the Greek students were gunning for me—I don't know why, maybe because I threw the first punch—and the next day, one of them arranged to have a meeting with Mike about it. Afterwards, Mike said to me, "We're going to have to get you out of here for a while." I packed a few things together quickly, the chauffeur drove me to the next town, and I stayed there for about four days till it all quietened down and I could come back.

When we were on location, it was always reassuring to be surrounded by familiar faces—and not just because we could rely on them if there was any trouble with the locals! Nine times out of ten, we'd know the guys on the set, from chippies, painters and sparks (electricians) to camera crews; they all loved Mike, and he liked me to fix it so that the people he was used to could work with him regularly. There were lots of our old friends on *Get Carter* (1971), directed by Mike Hodges, and also starring Britt Ekland and John Osborne: once again, I was the stunt arranger. I shall never forget the problems we encountered while the film was being set up, though. Early discussions about the project took place in Los Angeles, and Mike was dining with me and some friends in a famous restaurant there, the *Luau*, when the producer whose company was providing the financial backing for *Get Carter* arrived from London. He'd been downing a few drinks on the plane while watching *The Last Valley* on the in-flight entertainment channel—and, for some reason, he'd got annoyed about the German accent Mike used in that movie. So he walked into the restaurant, caught sight of Mike, and started having a go at him, shouting, right across the room, "What's with all this f***ing German dialogue?" Everyone was staring at him, and the situation was very embarrassing for Mike, especially as he was in company. I got up, had a word with the producer, and wheeled him away.

That went by...but a few months later, back in London, there was an almost identical incident involving the same man. It happened during a dinner that Michael Klinger, the principal producer of *Get Carter*, had arranged for Mike, Roger Moore, and about twenty more of us; he'd taken over the top floor of a West End restaurant for it. The producer who'd been at the *Luau* in LA was there as well. As I explained earlier, he was putting the money up for the production, and Klinger (who'd had the idea for the film, but wasn't a major producer in the same league as Harry Saltzman—in fact, he was a bit of a lad, who'd been involved with running the Compton Cinema Club in Soho, and once owned a hotel on the river in Richmond, quite close to where I live now) was relying on him. Once again, this guy had had a few drinks, and began being rude about Mike's German accent. Michael Klinger didn't know what to do: the bloke causing the trouble was a friend and colleague of his, and if Michael Caine had taken offence at his remarks, he might have decided to pull out of the film. Klinger turned to me and said, "Put the man in a cab, John," so I went over, got hold of him, and wheeled him downstairs. While we were waiting for a taxi outside the restaurant, he was leaning back on a parked car, still saying silly things. At this point, I didn't mince my words, and told him, "Look, this is the second time all this has happened, and you're giving me the hump. Do yourself a favour, get in the cab and eff off!" The cab came, we threw him in, and that was it.

Get Carter eventually went ahead without any major snags. It was shot around Newcastle, and one of the lads hired as an extra and a general help was a guy we nicknamed Tommy 'Twomoons': the producer and I knew him well, but it so happened that Mike didn't. Anyway, we were on the platform at King's Cross railway station in London, taking the train up to Newcastle, and Tommy was making himself busy. He'd got Mike's and Minda's luggage, as well as mine, and was pulling all the suitcases along on a big flat truck. All of a sudden, he ran over Minda's foot with it. Luckily, it just caught her and didn't go right over, but she screamed in pain, and Mike just went potty. "Who's that guy?" he asked me. "That's Tommy—he's a friend of the producer's," I answered. "Get him off the film!" said Mike. Poor old Tommy didn't know what to do, but I was able to sweeten it with the producer, and saved him from getting the sack.

Before setting up any stunts on a movie, I'd read through the script, mark out where the action was going to be, start to plan and get organised, and then show the director what I intended to do. For *Get Carter*, I actually spent a week in Newcastle prior to filming, seeking out locations and other things I'd need. A major item on my 'want list' was a Sunbeam Alpine convertible that would go into the water, with a body in its boot, in an important scene, and I went looking for one at a local breaker's yard, along with one of my stunt men. The place was surrounded by a big fence, but the gate was open, and we went in and told the owner what we were after. He took us up onto a ramp in a storage area to show us a suitable car. Quite suddenly, though, we had a serious problem: there was heavy security in the yard, and one of the staff thought we were intruders, shut the gate, and unleashed his guard dog at us. The animal, a big, very fierce Alsatian, was about to jump on me and the stunt man—but somehow I had the forethought and strength to grab the owner in my arms and use him as a shield against the dog. Luckily, they were able to chain it up again quickly, no one was injured...and I got the Sunbeam Alpine for the film!

One day, just after I'd completed my preliminary work for *Get Carter*, I came back from my lunch at Twickenham Studios to find an envelope addressed to me sitting on my desk. It contained the CV and photos of a talented young stunt man named Vic Armstrong, who was looking for a job on the film. Sadly, I already had everyone I needed, and couldn't make use of him—but he's gone on be immensely successful, and has won a string of awards: he's especially famous for his work with Harrison Ford on the *Indiana Jones* movies. It's a pity I didn't take him on...and if I'd done so, he might have been able to help me out in my own later career!

When I hired stunt men and women, I was usually looking for people who were good at *fights, cars* and *heights*. Years ago, when people staged fights in movies, a guy receiving a fake punch would have clapped his hands to make it sound like he'd taken a big hit, while gasping and groaning as if he'd been hurt; but nowadays, the crucial thing is to get the camera angles right, and have the actors' bodies in the right place. When you sling a punch, the guy you're pretending to hit needs to be behind you. Your fist actually goes past him, but it looks as though it's connected, and there'll be a sound effect to reinforce the illusion. In a face-slapping scene, though, the actor's hand really does have to make contact with the person being struck—but you can minimise the pain, and keep things looking real, if you slap someone's face with a cupped hand instead of an open palm.

There are standard 'tricks of the trade' for car crashes, too. If you're going to turn a car over, you build up a ramp, so that a vehicle can drive up one side of it and spin off. The ramp has to be camouflaged from the camera, as do the boxes that are used when staging crashes...though you do sometimes catch sight of them when they haven't been properly hidden. For stunts like these, it's essential to hire the best people for the job—guys like Frank Henson, whom we used to call 'Frank the Crash.' I called him in for *Get Carter,* along with my old friend Terry Plummer. There was one scene where I was driving the car, and Terry got into the passenger seat and said, "Come on, let's get out of here!" I arranged for another stunt man to try to jump in the back, but catch his leg in the seat belt, so that he got dragged along. It was a bit different, and I think it worked well.

I also called on the services of Derek Baker, an ex-Army guy who was a skilled parachutist. I'd met him years before, when we'd both been in the crowd as extras, and had worked together on the Beatles movies. Derek was always very keen: he had a huge bag full of his stunt gear, and he'd come up to me and ask, "What have you got for me today, John?" The other lads used to laugh at him, and they used to say to me, "Get him at it, get him at it!" He took part in the dance hall fight scene in *Get Carter,* in which he got thrown over a balcony. These days, people use airbags for falls like that—you just bring them onto the set, blow them up, and jump into them—but Derek had to make his own equipment, as we all did back then. He built up a pile of cardboard boxes, laid some mattresses over them, put a tarpaulin on top, and tied a rope around everything to keep the boxes in place when he landed on them. I had to tell him to drop the boxes down a bit, because they were at the same height as the balcony, and there was no room for the camera. Before the jump, he had to have a fight with two other guys, and I decided to get one of them to break a bottle over his head when he wasn't expecting it. Whack! The look on his face was priceless, and we were able to capture it on film.

Occasionally, things didn't work out. I'd flown a stunt man up to Newcastle to shoot a sequence where I wanted him to come off the top of a car park, but he wouldn't do it without using a rig that would have cost a lot of money, so I had to rearrange the scene. In situations like that, directors will often be egging the stunt men on...but if they're sensible, they'll only do the ones they feel are OK. Anybody who's stupid enough to say 'Yes' to everything can wind up being hurt, or even killed—which, sadly, several people have been.

And when you're planning or doing stunts, it's always a good idea to get to know the special effects guy you're collaborating with. You must be able to trust him, and be sure that what he's doing is safe, particularly if explosives will be going off when you're close by. One of my friends, Kit West, is one of the very best people in this field: we worked together on *Play Dirty* and *The Wilby Conspiracy*, and he went on to win an Oscar for his contribution to *Raiders of the Lost Ark* (1981).

In recent years, of course, movie stunting has been transformed by the use of Computer Generated Imagery (CGI), which is able to accomplish almost anything: actors can look like they're jumping off roofs, bouncing off cars...just like animated figures in a video game.

***

In my job—as a stunt arranger, and when I was looking after Mike—I had to be constantly on guard against anything going wrong, but sometimes you just can't foresee what will happen. At the end-of-picture party for *Get Carter*, I had minders put on the door, and all my stunt men were there. I was having a drink with them when somebody shouted out to me, "You'd better get in here." "What's going on?" I asked, and they told me, "Mike's had a problem." I found out that some guy, who hadn't been invited, and wasn't even part of the film unit, had climbed onto a stage where Mike was dancing with Minda, and touched him on the bum. Mike was shouting about it...so I went up, got hold of the guy who'd done it, threw him off and gave him a whack. Then I spoke to the minders and said, "How come you let him in? He's nothing to do with the film unit—and look what he's done! He's caused a problem."

We encountered something else completely unexpected when we were shooting *Kidnapped* (which, like *Get Carter*, came out in 1971): the production ran out of money while we were on location in Scotland. Apparently, when the lads working on the film phoned home, they were told by their wives that their salaries hadn't gone into their bank accounts. I double-checked with Mike's accountant, and found out that he wasn't getting paid either. The first assistant director came to me about the situation, and after I'd talked to Mike, we spoke to the producer, who was completely straight with us. He explained that they were in trouble and hadn't got any money, but that he'd see to it that the crew were paid. I think the technicians did eventually receive what they were owed, but I don't believe Mike did.

One good thing that came out of that trip to Scotland was my meeting with Greenmantle: two musicians, Billy Campbell and Jack Law, whom I heard one evening when they were performing at a hotel near one of our locations. I liked their sound—a nice, sort of country style—and could see that they were good-looking boys, who'd appeal to the girls. While I was chatting to them afterwards, I asked if anyone was managing them. They said no, and I told them I'd like to. So I took them on, brought them down to London, got them quite a few gigs (at smallish, but well-known venues like the *Half Moon* in Putney), and arranged a record deal for them with Philips. One day, after coming out of the label's offices near Marble Arch, I looked around and caught a glimpse of one of the Barclay twins—big businessmen who'd started out, like me, in Shepherd's Bush, where I often used to run into them. The twins, David and Frederick, always dressed very smartly, and with their dark hair they looked a bit like Italians. I'm not sure which of the two I saw that day in Marble Arch, but he recognised me and smiled...and then his Rolls-Royce came up, and he drove off.

Greenmantle's first single was released in 1974, and around that time, they had a show at the *Turk's Head* in Twickenham, near where I was living. The support group at the gig had overrun their allotted time by about twenty minutes, and weren't coming offstage, so my boys were asking me, "What's going on, John?" "I'll find out," I said, and after the support band had finally finished, I went outside to have a word with their manager. He started getting flash with me, and asking me who I thought I was. "This is who I am," I replied, and gave him a whack. I must have hurt him, because the police were called, and I remember running back into the *Turk's Head*, escaping through the kitchen, and heading back to my house, which was just nearby. I was long gone by the time the Old Bill arrived!

Later on, Greenmantle decided to expand their line-up, and brought in a drummer and another guitarist. Having to find accommodation for the two extra band members was making things hard for me, and I didn't really like the new sound they were going for. Eventually, they split up, which was a pity: Billy Campbell had a great voice, and Jack Law reminded me very much of George Harrison. It's good to know they're both still plugging away in the music business.

5: MY FINAL YEARS WITH MICHAEL

Three movies starring Michael were released in 1972: *Zee and Co.*, *Pulp*, and *Sleuth*. The first of these, directed by Brian G. Hutton, co-starred Elizabeth Taylor, and was mostly shot at Shepperton. Elizabeth was lovely, but Richard Burton, who was drinking pretty heavily at the time, was with her at the studios, and I remember a party there when he just came up to me and said, "Right, who can I have a row with?" "Why do you want to have a row?" I asked him— but that was just how he (and Richard Harris, as we've already seen) could be when they'd had a few. Mike himself used to drink quite a bit during the early stages of his career, probably because of his own worries and insecurities.

In *Sleuth*, he was cast alongside Laurence Olivier. There are stories about Olivier trying to upstage him, and I've already mentioned that Mike could be apprehensive when he appeared with really legendary names. However, I never saw any problems between the two of them —and it's well known that Olivier wrote to Mike at the start of the production, saying that he should always call him 'Larry', not 'Lord Olivier' or 'Sir Laurence.' Mike, Olivier, Joseph L. Mankiewicz (the director), and John Addison (who provided the music) all received Oscar nominations for their work on *Sleuth*.

In the stunts I did for Mike in this movie, his character, Milo, was wearing a clown costume. I found its big, long boots tricky to manage in one scene where I had to fall backwards from a ladder propped against the side of a building, after climbing about half-way up. Out of shot at the base were a couple of special effects guys, half-submerged below the studio stage. On "Action!" they whipped the bottom of the ladder so that it came crashing against the wall of the house. Everything went OK...except that the big clown boots made it awkward for me to keep my footing on the rungs. My left leg went through the ladder, and a rung caught me badly across the shin.

There could have been a more serious problem during another *Sleuth* stunt, where Milo falls down the stairs after being shot. Normally, I'd have been wearing padding for something like that—knee pads, elbow pads, and special pants that are padded at the back to protect the base of your spine. But for some reason, I didn't bother to on that day. It was silly not to, but I didn't want to hold things up. In fact I didn't rehearse the stunt at all: I reckoned I could just go for it, so they shouted "Action!" and down I went. The staircase had a bend to the right, and as I came around it, I whacked my head on the banisters. This time, though, my costume protected me. Its big headpiece acted as a cushion for my skull as I fell, and I didn't feel anything; if I hadn't had that helmet on, I certainly would have done. On both these stunts, we just kept the camera running, and were able to obtain the shots we needed—in fact, the crew didn't know anything had gone wrong until afterwards. We didn't stop...you just don't do that.

Pulp, with Mickey Rooney, and directed by Mike Hodges, was shot in Malta, where the manager of our hotel was a good friend of Sir Stanley Matthews, the famous English footballer who was living out there. I decided to set up a football match between the *Pulp* crew and a team led by my old pal Rocky Taylor, who was in Malta doing stunts for another film. A few days before the Sunday for which the match was scheduled, I met Sir Stanley through the hotel manager, and asked him, "Would you fancy a game of football with us?" Stanley replied, "Yes, love to!" and we arranged for the manager, who had a Rolls-Royce, to drop him off at the ground on the day. I said, "OK— but wait until we're all on the pitch, give us another five minutes after that, and then arrive."

So, come Sunday morning, all the players were waiting, Rocky was wanting us to kick off, and I was saying, "No, we're one man short, but he's definitely on his way, because I've had a phone call." At that moment, I saw the Rolls-Royce approaching, and shouted out, "There's our man! He'll be here right now." The car pulls up, and out gets Stanley, in all his gear. And you should have heard them all...Rocky was calling me everything! The funny thing was that even with Stanley on our side, we still got beaten, though he tried his very best, and was giving us all the gee-up: "Come on, lads, don't worry! They've had a few goals, but we'll get some..."

Pulp was one of the films where Jean, Vicky and Matthew were able to come and stay with me on location. Mike Hodges' then-wife was also called Jean, and our two families spent a good deal of time together, along with Michael Klinger, the producer: we were all out in Malta over Christmas, and the kids got spoilt rotten! On shooting days, Michael Caine would often join my family for a quick lunchtime snack at our hotel if he was able to get away from the set for an hour. And I shall always remember an incident that occurred at a swimming pool during our stay. The young son of Hodges' chauffeur had fallen into the pool, and sunk straight to the bottom, but my wife ran down the steps into the water, and was able to drag him out before any harm came to him.

There was a problem when Michael Caine and I were coming home from Malta after finishing location work for *Pulp*. We were actually on the runway, ready to take off, when the doors opened and two plain-clothes policemen came on board. They took me away, and held me for questioning. It turned out there was a suspect with the same name as me, and they thought he was trying to leave the country. It didn't take them long to realise they'd got the wrong person, so I was able to get back onto the flight and return to London.

When I arranged the stunts on Mike's next picture, *The Black Windmill* (1974), which also starred Donald Pleasence, Janet Suzman and John Vernon, and was directed by Don Siegel, I hired Terry Plummer (see Chapter 4) again, and he agreed to do what turned out to be a particularly hazardous fall; in fact, I'd already approached a couple of guys who didn't want to try it. It's in the scene where the baddie, who's being chased, runs into a windmill and tries to escape from his pursuers by climbing upstairs to the top. They fire their guns through the floor to kill him, and he drops through a trap door head first, then tumbles down a whole lot of steps like a dead body, turning around as he falls. The windmill's steps were just like a ladder, and we'd padded them all; but as he came down, Terry hit his head on every step, knocked himself out, and finished up in hospital. They kept him in for a couple of days, but thankfully, he was all right—and, once again, we managed to shoot the scene.

The Black Windmill was largely made in Kent and Sussex, but for *The Marseille Contract*, also released in 1974, and known as *The Destructors* in the USA, we started off on location in Marseille, continued filming right along the coast (taking in Saint-Tropez,

Cannes, Nice and Monte Carlo), and finished up in Paris. With lovely settings like that, it's little wonder that when Mike agreed to do the film, and the producers said they'd send him the script, he apparently replied, "Don't bother!" Anthony Quinn and James Mason were his co-stars; the director was Robert Parrish.

One stunt setup on the picture nearly went badly wrong. I'd made plans for a scene in the French capital where Mike's character, Johnny Deray, has to jump over a bridge and into a boat on the River Seine. Scaffolding and platforms were erected on the side of the bridge, so the camera could film Mike jumping over the parapet, and it would look as if he was going all the way down—but of course we'd cut, and it would be me, as his double, actually landing in the boat. Back then, the scaffolding they used out there was made of timber, not metal, and had to be lashed together. The cameraman wanted to inspect it, so he, the camera operator, the first assistant director, the director and I all stood on one of the platforms, which was about twenty feet high, and checked it out; then I jumped over the parapet so they could see how it would look. "Fine, lovely, terrific, OK!" said everyone. We climbed off, and were making our way back along the bridge when there was an almighty crash. The scaffolding had collapsed! When the workmen had built it up, it seems they hadn't lashed the wooden poles to the bridge, and so it all came away. We turned round and went white, because we'd all been on the structure just a moment before it fell.

When we were moving from location to location on *The Marseille Contract*, Mike asked me to "go out and find the best restaurants, wherever we are, so that we can have lunch at them instead of eating on the set." We had some marvellous food at these places (including oysters with hot cream, which I'd never tasted before), as well as the very best wines, sometimes costing over £100 a bottle. In Paris, while we were eating at a massive restaurant he knew—so large, it was like being in a railway station—he said to me, "I want to open a restaurant like this in London. When we get back, I'll have a look around and find somewhere suitable...and you'll be involved in it."

Mike realised his ambition in 1976, when he and Peter Langan opened Langan's Brasserie in Mayfair, with £25,000 of Mike's money —but by then, I was out of the picture. Things had started to change between the two of us during the making of *The Wilby Conspiracy*

(1975). He starred in it alongside Sidney Poitier and Nicol Williamson, and the director was Ralph Nelson. The location shooting took place in Kenya, where we stayed at the Mount Kenya Safari Club at Nanyuki, a lodge owned by actor William Holden. In the evenings, we'd usually be in the bar, though Mike himself wasn't down there on the day I'm talking about, and I was just having a drink with the lads—the sparks and other crew members. With us was a young English guy who'd been born in Africa and lived out there. He was a pilot, and we'd been using his plane in some of the scenes. The phone rang in the bar, and he picked it up and began chatting to the caller, who was clearly a woman. He started getting a little bit flash with her...and though he didn't know it, it was Nicol Williamson's wife, who must have told Nicol about the call as soon as she hung up. The next minute, he came storming down from their room, asking, "Who's that bastard who was talking to my wife on the phone?" The pilot, who, to give him credit, was certainly brave, owned up straightaway, and Nicol said, "Right: outside, you!" The guy got up and went out of the bar with Nicol—who turned to me as I was sitting there and said, "Come on, John!" So now I'm on duty again...

When they got outside, they started to have a terrible row, but I stepped in between them, pushed Nicol away, told him I'd take care of it, and started talking to the young guy. I said, "Now look. Don't be silly, because you could wind up getting hurt. If you damage Nicol, the film will stop, as we'll have lost an actor. And not only will you be in trouble about that, you're going to finish up with a right hiding from some of the sparks who won't be able to work and earn money while he's being patched up." I made him apologise, because otherwise Nicol would have borne a grudge, and things could have got nasty.

When we'd completed the location shoots, we were all set to fly home from Kenya and finish the film at Pinewood Studios, and were waiting in the VIP lounge at the airport in Nairobi: it had a corrugated roof, and was baking hot. Mike was accompanied by his wife, Shakira —he'd met her after breaking up with Minda, and they'd got married in 1973—and their daughter; and I had my wife, Jean, and Vicky and Matthew along with me. One of the stunt men, Bob Simmons, came up to me in the lounge and said, "We've got a problem, John. We've heard that our plane isn't leaving for London today, and our passports have been taken off us for some unknown reason." I told Mike, who said, "Well, get the producer. Where *is* the producer?" "He's back at the hotel—he's not here," I told him. Mike repeated, "Well, get him." I rang the hotel to ask the producer to come to the airport, but before long, Mike started to get worked up. He was pacing up and down and asking me, "Is he here yet? Is he here yet?"

When the producer eventually arrived in a car, I met him outside and said, "Mr. Caine wants to speak to you." "Yes," he replied, "in a minute." "Not in a minute," I told him, "I said now." So he went in to talk to Mike, and from where I was standing outside, near his car, I could look down into the VIP lounge. Suddenly, I saw my wife, Jean, nearly collapsing because of the intense heat in there. Mike's nanny saved her from falling and hitting the floor, and I rushed inside to see what was going on. In all the row, shouting and confusion, I just snapped—and the person I went for was the producer. I hit him, and I hit him again. The next thing I knew, one of the actors in the VIP lounge had put his arms around me, and locked me in so that I couldn't throw any more punches. He then wheeled me right away up to the other end of the airport.

I can't really remember what happened after that, because I was in such a rage that I'd lost it completely. I know we all had to go back to the hotel, and return to the airport the following day for our rescheduled flight to London. And when we got to Nairobi Airport the next morning, the first person there was the producer. He had two bunches of flowers in his arms, gave one of them to Shakira and the other to my wife, and then went to shake hands with me, and more-or-less apologise. But I just wouldn't have it. I wouldn't shake his hand. I'm really not a vicious person, not a fighter, and there are lots of times when I'll back away from an argument. But a situation like that one, when my wife and family are involved, and when people have been taking liberties or pulling rank, really upsets me.

A few weeks later, I was on the set at Pinewood with Mike. We were shooting a scene with Nicol Williamson when the main door opened, and in walked the film's three producers (who, incidentally, were all Americans), including the guy I'd hit. As soon as Nicol Williamson saw them, he stopped acting, looked over, and said, "Right, get those three off the set now, otherwise I'm going to finish what John Morris started!" I thought to myself, "Oh my God—he's put me right in it!" and said to Nicol, "Why on earth did you do that? It's all died down, and there's no need." "No," he replied, "I don't want them on the set." I still don't understand why Nicol said what he did, but reminding people of what had happened in Kenya certainly didn't make my situation any better. After all, hitting a producer on a film is really not a good idea. I may be the only person who's ever done such a thing!

It's important to say that these kinds of events are unusual. Most of the time, life on location is pretty peaceful, though there may be occasional dust-ups involving members of the crew. One or two riggers might start drinking heavily, and get themselves into a bit of trouble. You wouldn't want to upset riggers, because they're big guys. I've found that a lot of the problems are a result of people being away from home for a long time, getting bored, and missing their wives and children. And sometimes, the locations themselves aren't the kind of places where you'd choose to be, even though the crew members may be staying alongside the artists in decent accommodation. Working on a movie with big stars certainly isn't always glamorous and rosy.

***

A new chapter of Mike's life had begun when he married Shakira, and I think that, for understandable reasons, there was less room in it for some of the people he'd relied upon in the past. There were certainly far-reaching changes in his setup around this time. His chauffeur, his housekeeper, and his secretary all departed—and gradually, I started getting the impression that I wasn't wanted any more either. The last film Mike and I worked on together was *The Romantic Englishwoman* (1975), which also starred Glenda Jackson. By then, instead of buzzing around for him as I normally did, I'd arrive on the set, and there'd be nothing he'd want me to do. Not being part of things was hard for me to take, and it wasn't long before I decided to go.

My whole working life had revolved around Mike's, and splitting with him was quite a blow for me. Even when he'd spent time in the USA (for tax reasons, and when he was making American films that I wasn't involved with), I'd been kept on a retainer, and had stayed in London, reading scripts and doing other jobs for him. I'd been loyal, turned down approaches from other big names, and hadn't taken on other film projects when I could have done. And when a producer had wanted to make me his associate a few years earlier, I'd told him, "No, I'm happy where I am, thank you." Though I was well known in the business, I realised I was getting to an age where I couldn't really go on doing stunts for much longer, and began asking myself if I wanted to continue in movies at all now I wasn't with Mike. I had some hard decisions to make about my future, and while I was considering them, I just went into a shell, and stayed at home in Twickenham listening to music all day. I knew a big part of my life had come to an end...but ultimately, whatever sadness I had about that was far outweighed by the feeling that I'd been really privileged to work—so closely, and for so many years—with one of the all-time greats of British cinema, and to have assisted in the making of classic movies like *The Ipcress File*, *Funeral in Berlin*, *The Italian Job*, and *Get Carter*.

6: AFTER MICHAEL CAINE...

One of my first major ventures after splitting from Mike had its roots in a project I'd tried to get off the ground a few years before. I'd been a Queens Park Rangers supporter since I was twelve years old (so are my son Matthew, and his sons Max, Joel and Freddie). I knew Phil Parkes, the team's goalkeeper, and often used to go and watch them at their ground in Loftus Road. I'd taken Mike to a match there in the early 1970s: they were playing Leeds, whose fans had a reputation for being a bit heavy at that time. When QPR won, the Leeds supporters came rushing across the pitch, and it looked like it was all going to go off. Mike was worried for his life, but I told him not to be scared, took him into the Players' Bar, where he was safe, and introduced him to Phil. Around this time, I'd had an idea for a TV documentary about the history of football, going right back to the early days when players didn't have a ball, but used to kick a pig's bladder around. I was going to get Roger Moore to be the programme's executive producer, and had a contact in America who was very interested in it. Sadly, the show never got made, probably because I was away on a film with Mike.

I'd kept in touch with Phil Parkes, and in 1976, he and I went into partnership and set up a sports shop in the St. Margarets area of Twickenham. It was called 'Phil Parkes Sports Ltd.', and we rented its premises from Millets, the outdoor clothing retailers. The opening, on 22nd April that year, was quite an occasion: the entire QPR team was there, including their manager, Dave Sexton, and I hired some models dressed in football shorts to serve drinks and food to the guests. The crowds we attracted were so large that they blocked the main street, and the police were very annoyed that I hadn't notified them in advance. Gerry Francis, the team's captain, was going to perform the opening ceremony, but he got held up, so the comedian Leslie Crowther, who lived just around the corner, stepped in and made the announcement for us.

It was good having the shop, and though it required quite a big commitment from me, I had assistants, and was able to get away whenever I needed to. I remember one morning, when I'd parked my car, and was going across to open up, I noticed a guy with long hair looking into the window. As I put the key in the front door, I turned around, and saw that it was Paul McCartney! He said hello—I hadn't been in touch with him for some time—and I asked what he was doing there. He explained that he was rehearsing at Twickenham Studios, had heard that I'd got the shop, and decided to drop in. We had a bit of a chat, and he said, "Come round later for a cup of tea at the studios." I don't know why, but for some reason I didn't go—which I've always regretted, as Paul was always such a nice guy, and it was really kind of him to come round.

Phil Parkes used to help out at the shop most days after he'd finished training. Having him there was important, as his name was over the door, and people expected to see him. I think he found it enjoyable, and the shop might have survived if it hadn't been for a couple of rival stores, including a big supermarket, that set up in the area and slaughtered us, trade-wise. A friend of Phil's then appeared on the scene: he wanted to get involved with the business and expand it...but it turned out that it was Phil, not me, that he wanted to work with. The three of us had a meeting, and the guy was talking about opening a new shop, with Phil, in Shepherd's Bush, when I stopped him and said, "This is a limited company. You do know that, don't you? You can do what you like with Phil, but you can't use the 'Phil Parkes Sports Ltd.' name, because I'm not interested in going with you." He and Phil did go into business together under a different name in Shepherd's Bush, but it wasn't a success...and in 1993, I decided to sell the original shop in St. Margarets.

I started several other businesses during this period. I bought a hairdressing salon for my daughter, who'd just qualified as a hair stylist, and I also took on a franchise, with my son, for a new method of carpet-cleaning from the States. He and I set up another company that laid patios and driveways in different colours, using epoxy resin and trowelled-in quartz stones. We had a stand at the Hampton Court flower show, and also got a contract to do the floors for the back staircases at the Shepherd's Bush Hilton. But I never completely turned my back on film and TV: they were still in my blood. I worked as a line producer on a project at Shepperton, in collaboration with two Welshmen who'd been running a video shop. They'd decided they could make films better than the ones they were renting out, and were hoping I could open a few doors for them, and introduce them to people.

After that, my old friend Terry Plummer put me in touch with a company that wanted me to help set up films. They knew I had contacts, so they more-or-less stuck me up as an associate producer. They were going to be the main producers, but would still need to obtain money, and make a deal with one of the big majors to get distribution...without which, of course, you're nowhere. They'd rented five offices at Pinewood, and I began getting things lined up for them. However, they didn't seem to understand much about the business; and one day, I came into the Pinewood offices to find that all the desks had been cleared. The paperwork, the computers, and everything else had vanished, and while I was there, the phone rang. It was the studio manager, saying, "We'd like you to leave today." When I asked him why, he told me there'd been a police raid the night before, and that my company's main man, who was a gangster, had been arrested. For some time, there'd been an undercover police officer in the next-door office to ours, investigating the guy. She was a very good-looking Indian lady, who never seemed to be doing very much. I'd met her and talked to her, and when I'd asked her about her job, she'd told me she was involved in producing films, and putting money into them. "Well, I'd like to have a chat with you, then!" I'd said. And she was the Old Bill! It turned out that they'd been bugging our offices, and had taped over 400 hours of our meetings and conversations. Some of the material was used at the gangster's trial, and he eventually received a ten-year prison sentence.

I was able to move the remnants of the company—myself, a secretary, and an actor—to Shepperton, where we continued to work for a while; but once again, things didn't work out as I'd hoped, and I began to wonder if I should forget about show business once and for all.

It was one of my friends, who'd worked in films for years, and was a member of the same karate club as me, who said, "Instead of hanging about doing nothing, why don't you come back into the business on the props side? You know what it involves, and it won't take you long to pick it up." I thought about it, and decided to give it a go. So I became a 'prop master,' mostly doing commercials—which made very good money but involved lots of hard graft. At the start of a project, you're called in by the art director and shown the script. Then you mark out the props you'll need, which the producers will supply. At the shoot itself, it's your job to keep everything organised and looking right, and you're also responsible for continuity—so if, in a particular scene, someone drinks from a cup or throws something onto the floor, you have to refill the cup or clean up the mess before they reshoot it.

I wasn't accustomed to the hours: as a prop master, you're the first person on the set in the morning, and the last off. You're usually on your own, and when everybody else has gone, you're still there, clearing up. Once, when I'd finished at about 11 o'clock at night, I had a two-hour journey back home, and it had been such a long day that I was nodding off at the wheel of the big Volvo estate car I drove to and from the locations. The back of the Volvo was loaded with all the gear that I might need: it was essential to have everything to hand, as there wouldn't be time to go out and buy a particular item during a shoot (even if there happened to be shops nearby), and you'd be in big trouble with the director if he called for something and you hadn't got it. Among the things I used to take with me was an old-fashioned beekeepers' gun: it would originally have been used to smoke out bees, and you'd load it with charcoal before lighting it and pumping it up to get it going. Smoke effects were really in vogue at one time— they gave a grainy, mysterious atmosphere that loads of cameramen were after—but the health and safety people wouldn't allow that sort of smoke gun any more, because it's a fire hazard and produces fumes; nowadays people have electric ones.

I'll never forget a fire problem we had on a commercial I did with a mate called Bert; he'd been in the prop business longer than me, and we often worked together. One day, we were on a set that had a big walk-in fireplace, and a fire with a calor gas cylinder unit at the back. I said to Bert, "You stand inside the fireplace, and I'll go round the back and switch the gas on. When it's on, I'll tell you, and you can light it." I went and turned on the gas, and called out to Bert—but for some reason, he couldn't hear me. So I shouted louder, "Bert, the gas is on!" And all of a sudden: 'Boom!' The gas had built up in the fireplace, and as soon as Bert lit it, it exploded, burning away all his hair and his sideburns, as well as blowing off the cap he always wore. Fortunately, he wasn't badly hurt...and I couldn't stop laughing.

The other items I carried included a 'Henry' vacuum cleaner to suck up any spilled water, lots of different tools and cleaning materials (such as sprays to get fingerprints and dust off mirrors and glass), a bag of white gloves, and various kinds of sticky tapes—double-sided ones, Gaffa tape—which we used all the time. When I went onto a set in the morning, I'd set up a table with all this kit on it: it was like a portable workshop, and sometimes, if there were parking restrictions, I had to unload everything, and then leave my car several streets away.

As well as the commercials, I did a few movies, both as a prop master (who, on a feature film, would be in the office, organising everything), and as the 'standby props' man who's actually there on the set during the shoot. I was standby props for *A Private Function* (1984), a comedy about a pig, which we filmed in Yorkshire; it starred Michael Palin, Richard Griffiths and Maggie Smith, had a screenplay by Alan Bennett, and was directed by Malcolm Mowbray. When you're standby props for a picture, keeping track of continuity is an even bigger job than it is on a commercial. You'll be watching every move the actors make—keeping an eye on where they put down their teacups in a scene, and on what they do with their lighters after they've lit a cigarette—and you'll have an assistant, who does the running around for you.

On another project around this time, I was working on location in Morocco. We had British caterers providing our food, and one day, I went down to the local town with them, and had a look around its market. The red meat on sale there was hanging up in the open, with flies all over it—and I asked the caterer, "Where do you buy your meat from?" "I get it here, downtown," he told me. "Oh, do you?" I replied. I just couldn't believe he'd use meat when it was in that sort of condition, and that was it for me: I've never eaten red meat since, from that day to this. I can't even stand the smell of it cooking, though I still enjoy chicken.

A little later, I was hired as prop master for a movie being shot around the west coast and Western Isles of Scotland. There were no big hotels in the area that the crew could use, but I'd found a convenient flat for myself. About four or five weeks into the film, I'd arranged to bring Jean and the children to stay there with me, when suddenly, the production manager came along and said, "You've got to give up that flat." I explained that my family were booked to come and join me there, but he told me I had to leave the flat. I knew that if I was forced to share accommodation with one of the crew, there'd be no room for Jean and the kids, so I asked, "Who's having my flat?" "The producer's coming up from London, and he'll be staying there," he replied.

I'd come across this particular producer before, when I'd worked with him on a commercial; he'd only just got into films, and the Scottish one was to be his first. We were all out on the set the day he arrived, and when I caught sight of him I got the hump because he'd taken over my flat...just saw red, went potty, and went over and hit him. I remember a couple of sparks grabbing me and holding me back. Of course, that was the second producer I'd hit, and it's really something you don't do in the film business. I got thrown off the film immediately, and sent home: the production manager called me to one side and said, "That's it. You're finished." "Good!" I said, and went back to pack my bags. I'm sorry to say that some of the crew—people I knew very well, and had often worked with—just didn't want to know me after all this: I was bad news. And after I got back to London, I was told the producer I'd hit suffered from meningitis (which I obviously didn't know), and that I might have killed him. The production company were threatening to sue me if the guy's health was affected by the fight, but he was OK, and I heard nothing more about it.

There was a similar situation in Gibraltar, when I was standby props on another film. I'd already been out there looking at locations and making notes of what we would need, but when we started shooting the movie, I fell out with the art director. I thought he was being a bit flash, and trying to drop me in it. I had a pal on the production, who'd got me the job, and he let the art director know that I wasn't happy. I'll never forget what happened next. I saw the art director on the quayside in Gibraltar, shouted out to him, "I want a word with you," and he ran away! I started chasing after him...but then I suddenly thought, "Oh, God! What am I doing? This is stupid.

I'm running after this guy, I only want a word with him, and he's running for his life!" So I just stopped, and decided to leave it alone.

I carried on with commercials when there wasn't any film work, and, to be honest, it suited me to operate by myself, without the need for assistants. I had an agent, who'd phone me up and offer me a week or two weeks at Shepperton or Pinewood; and sometimes advertising agencies, or particular art directors who liked me, would call me direct, and ask for me on their next production. I did some great ads over the years. Some of them were like scaled-down movies, and among the stars who appeared in them were Bruce Forsyth, Joanna Lumley, Frank Bruno (a lovely guy), and Jonathan Ross (whose ways and looks really reminded me of Michael Caine). So I met a range of nice people, including technicians and producers who'd be making commercials between their film jobs, because the money was so good. There were other perks, too: on ads like the ones for Woolworths, there'd sometimes be a whole lot of good stuff going free at the end of the shoot!

I finally stopped making commercials in the early 1990s. Everything was getting harder: even the parking was a problem at some small studios, and production standards were certainly dropping...as they've continued to in recent years. I don't know who dreams up today's ads, but I think some of them are diabolical! And, in the film industry in general (as I found out when people cold-shouldered me after I'd hit that producer in Scotland), quite a few people on the crew side are so anxious to work on a producer's or director's next project that they'll do anything to get the job—run about like blue-arsed flies, never step out of line. I could never be like that: I am what I am, and if you don't like it, sod it.

Looking back over my career in films, there are some sad memories. One of the stunt men I worked with on *The Quiller Memorandum* in the mid-60s—a really likeable guy, who hadn't been doing stunts very long, but was getting quite a bit of work—got killed, a few years later, on a job where he had to fall back from a ladder at the top of a house onto a pavement. He was using boxes and mattresses, as they did in those days when stunt rigging was lighter than it is now; but it all went wrong, his head whiplashed back onto the concrete, and that was the end of him.

And there's another tragic story I recall: a very good pal of mine,

Mike Carter (a nice guy who'd been in the crowd with me, as well as doing stunts), didn't like heights, and was losing work as a result. He'd failed to get a stunting job on a Bond film that was being made at the time, and some of the other lads used to wind him up about it. He was renting a room in Bedford Park, near where Jean and I were living, and one day, when he'd been to visit us and the children, and was about to leave, I asked him if he'd like to meet up later. "No, I've got something to do," he replied. He went off, and that was the last time I saw him.

A few days afterwards, some of the guys who lodged in the same house as he did came round to ask me if I'd seen him. When I said I hadn't, they got worried: there'd been no sign of him, but his car was still parked outside the house. We tried to get into his room, but couldn't open the door. What had happened was that he'd pushed a chest of drawers up against it, laid out his watch and his other valuables on top, put a pillow down on the floor by the fire, and gassed himself. It seems that things had just got too much for him.

Nearly everything else about all those years in the business has been enjoyable—and often very funny in retrospect, even though it may have been surprising or shocking at the time. There was a memorable incident on *Play Dirty*, when I'd finished shooting for the day, and needed to get back to the hotel. A car drew up, and the driver agreed to give me a lift, so I got into the front seat. In the back was an Arab guy who was in charge of handling the snakes we needed for the movie; he kept them in a straw basket, with a cloth over the top to stop them getting out. He also had scorpions and spiders, which were required for a different scene. He didn't speak very good English, but when I asked him, "Where's the snakes?" he said, "There, in the basket." I realised the things were in the car with us, and thought, "Oh, my God..." Anyway, on the journey back, I felt something touch my leg—so I jumped up, hitting my head on the roof of the car, and flung my arms out, catching the driver. "What's up?" he called out. "Those poxy snakes are in the back, and I think one of them's caught my leg," I shouted. I thought I'd had it! The driver stopped the car, and we had a look, but it turned out that all the snakes were still in the basket, and I never found out what it was that I felt in that car.

And I shall never forget the day I came across a couple of painters heading for the production office at a studio, absolutely smothered in paint. It was running down their faces, and all over their clothes: I think they'd started off just having a laugh by flicking paint at each other; but then, as it escalated, out came the cans, and "Whee! Get hold of that!" They were probably going to be sacked for it, because you don't need that sort of behaviour on a film set. It just isn't done, but it does happen...though, if we're talking about things you shouldn't do, I reckon that hitting a producer is just about top of the list!

Terrible life I've had, haven't I? I always seem to have been getting into trouble. No wonder nobody phones me any more...

SOME OF MY STUNTING COLLEAGUES

Over the years, I've worked with many of the very finest stunt men and stunt women in the business. Several of my closest friends and associates are listed here: sadly, quite a few are no longer with us.

Derek Baker
Mark Boyle
George Cooper
Michael Douglas
Eddie and Sadie Eden
Dorothy Ford
Richard Graydon
Rémy Julienne
Keith Peacock
Terry Plummer
Bob Simmons
Rocky Taylor

POSTSCRIPT - I

I'm going to end this book with two of the very few movie press releases that were written about me during my years with Michael Caine. First, here's one from Bataan in the Philippines: it dates from 1969, when Too Late The Hero *was being shot.*

John Morris, Michael Caine's stunt double in European films ranging from *The Ipcress File* to *Play Dirty*, makes his featured motion picture debut as an actor in Robert Aldrich's *Too Late The Hero*, now on location here.

Morris plays the key role of wounded British Army Captain Trevor, an 'expendable' in the $8-million action drama of World War II in the Pacific. Caine and Cliff Robertson are starred. Henry Fonda is special guest star.

A former freelance who once stunt-doubled for Roger Moore and John Lennon, Morris later joined Caine's London production staff and accompanied the star to the Philippines location of *Hero* as a production aide.

Caine, who had urged Morris to enter acting ranks, and producer-director Aldrich persuaded the husky six-footer to play the Trevor role. He does not, however, appear in a scene with Caine, but with co-stars Harry Andrews and Denholm Elliott.

To give Morris's acting debut full value, Aldrich provided the clincher: he assigned a stunt double to perform long-distance running shots, and saved former stuntman Morris for close-ups.

POSTSCRIPT - II

This earlier press release dates from 1966, when Michael and I were in Helsinki, working on Billion Dollar Brain.

STAND-IN AND STAR ARE COCKNEYS,
LOOK-A-LIKES AND FRIENDS

Stories about stars' stand-ins are sometimes frowned upon by film publicists—the limelight is for the star—but the story of Johnny Morris, stand-in for Michael Caine, is different, refreshing and worth telling.

Morris, who was once John Lennon's stand-in, is now in Finland in his capacity as stand-in for Michael, whose new film—Harry Saltzman's *Billion Dollar Brain*—is location shooting here.

"Michael," says Johnny Morris, "is not just my employer, he is my most valued friend. He is a wonderful person to work for. He is considerate and carries his fame lightly. He is the only actor I've ever worked with who has actually fetched *me* a cup of tea!"

Both men have similar backgrounds—for example, both are London cockneys—and they have almost identical physical characteristics. Like Caine, Morris is 6' 1" tall. He has the same weight, the same colour hair and skin, and, like Michael, wears glasses. Both are 33. Yet there is this significant difference. Michael's personality is extrovert, whereas Johnny's is reticent, but it is a difference between stand-in and star that makes for a successful professional relationship.

John Morris was born in Shepherd's Bush, London, a section on the other side of the river from the Elephant & Castle, which was Michael's home ground. Nevertheless, both areas are definitely 'working class,' a term rarely used in England where it is fashionable to imagine that class-consciousness is dying. 'The Bush' and 'The Elephant' breed Londoners, and that's what both Johnny and his 'guv'nor' are.

Morris has had some success as an actor himself—he played a small part in *Those Magnificent Men In Their Flying Machines*, and in *The Saint* and *Gideon's Way* television series. But finding the going hard, he attended an audition for the job of stand-in for Beatle John Lennon. He got it, and worked with Lennon on *A Hard Day's Night* and *Help!* But for the past three years he has been working for Michael—on *The Ipcress File*, *Funeral in Berlin*, and now *Billion Dollar Brain*, the three films in which Caine plays Harry Palmer, the reluctant cockney spy, and on *Alfie* and *The Wrong Box*.

For John Morris—who is married and has a young daughter—the work has meant extensive overseas travel, the ability to buy a new home in fashionable Thames-side Chiswick, and an enduring admiration for a man who is now an international star.

Some photographs of me from the 1960s, sent out to potential clients by the agent who handled my modelling assignments. My measurements, hair colour and hat and glove size were shown on the back.

Here, we're rehearsing the scene from *Play Dirty* in which I get flung out of an ambulance; you can see the vehicle on the far right of the second photo. Director André de Toth (with the eye patch) is showing me and actress Vivian Pickles—whose stunt double was Sadie Eden—what he wants from us. I think Vivian was glad I'd given her some judo lessons before we started work!

In costume alongside Michael Caine (r), who starred as Captain Douglas in *Play Dirty*. The movie was set in North Africa during World War II.

Me and Michael outside his caravan (today's stars would be provided with much larger, more luxurious ones!) on location for *Play Dirty*.

Getting ready for a scene for *Play Dirty*. I'm brandishing the gun; the bearded guy clutching its magazine is my old friend Kit West, a special effects artist and future Oscar winner.

Another *Play Dirty* photo: I'm relaxing at the wheel of a heavily laden Army truck.

Conditions during shooting for *Too Late The Hero* in the Philippines were gruelling. Director Bob Aldrich's shorts and plimsolls must have been far more comfortable than what the actors had to wear—though, as you can see from the next picture, I needed some extra fake sweat for this scene!

L-R: Lance Percival, Ronnie Fraser and Michael Caine alongside me at Taipei Airport during a four-day break from filming *Too Late The Hero*.

The Olongapoo Patrol

John Morris after paying more than four visits to Olongapoo City, and thus being able to show a clean Bill of Health? Is now entitled to become a life member of the above patrol.

Signed:

Percy Herbert!

Members of the 'Olongapoo Patrol' kept an eye on each other when visiting Olongapo City. This is my certificate of membership, signed by Mike, Ronnie Fraser, Percy Herbert and others.

I took the next two photos of Mike in costume as 'The Captain' while we were shooting *The Last Valley* in Austria.

A picture of me in Newcastle, taken while I was working as the stunt arranger for *Get Carter*.

A light-hearted moment on the set of *Get Carter* in Newcastle. Mike holds the clapperboard, I have my hands on the camera, and stunt man Derek Baker is sitting on the right.

Jack Law (l) and Billy Campbell (r) of Greenmantle, the Scottish band I managed in the 1970s.

A signed photo of me with Sir Laurence Olivier, who starred alongside Michael Caine in *Battle of Britain* and *Sleuth*.

In the stunts I did for Mike in *Sleuth*, his character, Milo Tindle, was dressed as a clown. They were pretty strenuous, and I appear to be taking a well-earned rest here!

A stunt from *Sleuth*, shown in sequence. In this first photo, I'm climbing up the ladder to get into position...

I then discuss what I'm going to do, while the lights are adjusted.

Action! I'm falling backwards with the camera rolling.

Staircase falls, though part of a stunt man's stock-in-trade, are tricky and potentially dangerous. Here, Olivier's character in *Sleuth*, Andrew Wyke, is behind Milo as he starts to come down the stairs.

Is Milo dead? Having apparently been shot by Wyke on the stairs, I've fallen down to the ground floor.

On the set of *Pulp* with the great Mickey Rooney.

Here, I'm walking alongside Don Siegel, director of *The Black Windmill*. He said he wanted me to be his associate producer on a future project, but sadly, it never came about.

Filming a stunt in a winery for *The Marseille Contract*. I'm standing beside the barrels, and Mike can be seen towards the right of the picture, next to the crew member with the clipboard and white boots.

A group of local kids in Kenya, photographed with me during shooting for *The Wilby Conspiracy*. The movie couldn't be made in South Africa, where the story is set, because of its anti-apartheid subject matter.

To Johnny
Good Things To
a Good Person
always

Sidney Poitier

Sidney Poitier, who co-starred with Michael Caine in *The Wilby Conspiracy*, signed this photo for me.

A dinner party in Kenya at the end of shooting for *The Wilby Conspiracy*. Left to right in the foreground are Shakira Caine, Michael Caine, Dennis Selinger (Mike's agent), me and my wife Jean.

Police supervise crowds of autograph hunters outside the shop.

Two photos from the *Richmond & Twickenham Times*, showing the celebrations that marked the opening of 'Phil Parkes Sports', which I co-owned, in Twickenham on Thursday 22nd April 1976.

This photo of me, and the one on the next page, were taken in 2014 by my friend Lynne Cahill.

INDEX